Bodhipaksa

Vegetarianism

WINDHORSE PUBLICATIONS

179.73 BOD

Published by Windhorse Publications
11 Park Road, Birmingham, B13 8AB

Printed by Interprint Ltd
Marsa, Malta
Cover design: Dhammarati
Detail of cow © Stephen McMillan
courtesy Bodega Landmark Studio, Bodega, California CA94922
Detail of leaf © Photodisc

British Library Cataloguing in Publication Data:
A catalogue record for this book is available from the British Library.
ISBN 1 899579 15 x

Since this work is intended for a general readership, Pali and Sanskrit
words have been transliterated without the diacritical marks which
would have been appropriate in a work of a more scholarly nature.

CONTENTS

Preface 1

Introduction 6

1 The Sufferings of Farm Animals 10

2 Why are we Beastly to Animals? 25

3 Buddhist Ethics 33

4 The Benefits of Vegetarianism 50

5 Commonly Asked Questions 63

6 Did the Buddha Eat Meat? 73

7 Meat and Metta 80

Conclusion 87

Notes 89

Further Reading 97

Index 99

In fond memory of my friends Clive Baillie (1962–96)
and Julie Boucher (1963–96), who with their
typical kindness and generosity lent me their house
in which to start writing this book;
their computer on which to do hours of research;
and the tin-opener, with which to feed the cat.

About the Author

Bodhipaksa was born Graeme Stephen in 1961 in Dundee. He graduated from the Veterinary School of the University of Glasgow, having inherited a love of animals from his grandfather. It was during his training as a veterinary surgeon that he became a Buddhist. A few months later, a visit to an abattoir in the course of his studies convinced him to become a vegetarian.

Since then he has worked in a Buddhist printing business, and also in community education for four years. He was ordained in 1993 and given the name Bodhipaksa, which can be translated as 'Wings of Enlightenment'. After that he ran a retreat centre in the Scottish highlands for three years before moving to Edinburgh to teach meditation and Buddhism.

Bodhipaksa is currently studying for a master's degree at the University of Montana, investigating Buddhist approaches to work and economics, and teaching at the Rocky Mountain Buddhist Center.

PREFACE

This is the first in a series of books on different aspects of Buddhist life. What is meant by a Buddhist life? When I tell people I am a Buddhist, that my name is a Buddhist name given to me at my ordination, I meet many responses: 'You don't look like a Buddhist,' 'What are you allowed to do?' and 'That's all very well in an ideal world but what about the real world?' as though to live a Buddhist life one would need to look and dress in a particular way (with shaved head and robe?), have a restricted lifestyle imposed by some authority, or be living out a pleasant but irrelevant and unrealistic dream. That is not the kind of life I lead – nor is it the life of those many Buddhists with whom I have been practising for the last twenty years, nor would we choose to live such a life; in fact some aspects of such a life would be anathema to the practice of Buddhism.

So the practice of Buddhism does not necessitate one particular lifestyle – in which case, why this series of books? The authors, who are all Western Buddhists, examine the potential of the Buddhist life as they live it, invite those with an interest in Buddhism to explore that potential with them, and, in the process, correct a few misunderstandings about Buddhism and Buddhist lives.

The importance of the theme 'living a Buddhist life' lies in the fact that the practice of Buddhism is for the whole person. It concerns our actions of body, speech, and mind – no aspect of our life is exempt. The teaching of the Buddha has been summed up in a single phrase, 'actions have consequences'. Our thoughts, words, and deeds all have their effect in the world, for good or ill, creating either happiness or suffering.

Unskilful actions – those proceeding from states of mind based on craving, ill will, and ignorance – create suffering. Skilful actions create happiness and proceed from states of mind based on generosity, love, and wisdom. To be able to recognize and distinguish mental states we need to be aware. So a Buddhist lives, or attempts to live, with awareness, and imbues, or tries to imbue, every area of life with these qualities of generosity, love, and wisdom. It is not an easy task but it is one that gives rise to many benefits.

Buddhist practices – of meditation, ritual, and study of the Dharma (the Buddha's teaching) – are undertaken in order to develop greater awareness and friendliness. In addition, our everyday activities provide infinite opportunities to practise and to change ourselves. In this way we guide and direct the lives we create, both individually and collectively. With consistent effort we can reach the point of Insight, direct experience of things as they really are.

Vegetarianism is a good subject with which to start the series, because food is so basic to our lives. We all eat. In the West, most of us have a great deal of choice in what we eat. What we choose to eat can also be challenging as we can be very attached to certain foods, either out of habit or out of desire. I was raised on the traditional 'meat and two veg' of the average British family. Influenced by the hippie ethos of my generation I became more inclined towards vegetarian food until two experiences finally convinced me to adopt a wholly vegetarian diet. One was going 'back to the land' on a self-sufficient farm in Ireland, where we lived off the vegetarian produce that we grew, and were proud to have to purchase only rice, salt, and tea. Following this, I travelled in India for a year and was very influenced by seeing the majority, rather than the minority, of the population living by tradition or choice on a vegetarian diet. Since that time, thirty years ago, I have been healthily and happily vegetarian.

Coming into contact with Buddhism ten years later gave me a wider and more profound context within which to affirm my decision. The first of the five Buddhist precepts observed throughout the Buddhist world is 'I undertake the training principle of abstaining from harming living beings.' Positively formulated, this can be expressed as a commitment to act with loving kindness. This precept embraces all living beings in its scope, those of the human realm as well as animals, birds, and creatures of the sea. As well as abjuring the killing or harming of these beings, it also means affirming, encouraging, and supporting all life in whatever form. Adopting a vegetarian diet is a clear and immediate way of practising and demonstrating this affirmation of life.

Bodhipaksa, having qualified as a veterinary surgeon prior to becoming a member of the Western Buddhist Order, has the advantage of being able to examine and write about vegetarianism from both these perspectives. His introduction to the subject lays bare the sufferings inflicted on animals for the sake of human consumption. He questions why we are prepared so readily to inflict this suffering, looks at the views and myths behind this relationship of human beings and animals, and examines the ethical conflict that many people experience between their conscience and their actions in this area. Contrasted with this is the Buddhist perspective – that all life is interconnected and that the more our actions reflect this truth and the more we live in accord with reality, the greater will be our sense of harmony and happiness.

We often wish to change the world. Buddhism teaches that we need to start by changing ourselves – but it also demonstrates how, through the cumulative effect of the actions of individuals, we can shape the world in which we live. Through his discussion of vegetarianism, Bodhipaksa shows us how the Buddha's teaching had a profound effect on the habits of almost a third of the world's population with the spread of vegetarianism. In so doing, he demonstrates that by living a Buddhist life, imbued with Buddhist values, we too can be an active force for change in the world.

Maitreyi
Tiratanaloka
Wales
April 1999

INTRODUCTION

I'd never considered being a vegetarian before – but then I'd never seen an animal being slaughtered, either. My class of veterinary students was touring an abattoir in the third year of our training, and we were being shown how animals are killed. The pig chosen for slaughter was shot in the head with a captive-bolt pistol, had its throat sliced with a knife, and died in a pool of blood on a white tiled floor. It took only a few seconds.

Many people – millions, even – have given up meat in recent years. Vegetarians are no longer a tiny minority but make up a significant portion of the population of the UK. In other parts of the Western world we see the same trend taking place. This represents a major change in eating habits in the last half-century, and a change in our ethical relations with the animal world. As with most changes, there has been some confusion. Some advertisements claim that meat is essential for health and others that it kills us. Some advertisements tell us we need 'Meat to Live'; others that 'Meat is Murder.'

It can be hard to take an objective look at the subject of meat-eating. Even thinking about changing a long-held habit – and we may have been eating meat since we were babies – can be difficult. Our friends might eat meat and see no problem in what they do, and it is not easy to be different from those we are close to. On the other hand the issue of animal suffering can stir strong emotions. This can be useful, but it can also make it harder to be clear about the issues involved. Sometimes it seems easier not to think about the subject at all! But if you've picked up this book then presumably vegetarianism is something you're looking into, and even thinking of taking up yourself.

Can Buddhism help in sorting out the ethical issues involved? Or is the picture in the Buddhist world just as confused – perhaps even more so? At the opening of a new Tibetan temple in the UK, the tables were laden with chicken and other meats for the assembled guests. In a Chinese monastery, the monks are strictly vegetarian, and the laity eat vegetarian food on special occasions. The Dalai Lama eats meat, although other Buddhists think that eating flesh is a breach of the most fundamental rule of Buddhist ethics.

It is my belief that Buddhist ethics does support the adoption of a vegetarian, even vegan, diet, and this book aims to encourage those who eat meat to become vegetarian. I hope it will be of particular interest to those who are starting to take Buddhism seriously and are considering the implications that Buddhist principles may have for their lives. I also hope it has something to offer those who may not consider themselves Buddhists but who want to learn what perspectives Buddhist ethics has to offer. If long-established Buddhists, vegetarian or not, find any benefit from reading these words, that is all to the good.

Buddhism encourages us to develop a deeper and more compassionate relationship with the world in which we live. Ideally – Buddhism teaches – we should strive to take responsibility for the effects of our actions so that our lives result in as little harm as possible, and we do as much good as we can. Of course, if we don't know the results of our actions, it is hard, if not impossible, to take responsibility in this way. Particularly in the West we are 'protected' from such an awareness where meat-eating is concerned, because those who produce meat know that many of us would be reluctant to eat it if we knew the unpleasant details of its production.

As a step in learning more about the effects of our actions, we'll take a trip down to the farm and the slaughterhouse to see how animals live and die. This will help us make a more informed choice about whether we want to support those activities. We will investigate the basis of Buddhist ethics, and how it relates to meat-eating. We'll look at some of the most commonly asked questions that arise in regard to becoming vegetarian, and consider whether vegetarianism is healthy. We'll also look at some of the positive consequences of adopting a vegetarian diet – for ourselves and for the planet we inhabit. We will also examine whether the Buddha ate meat, and if he did, whether this provides grounds for us doing so.

But first, to fundamentals....

1

THE SUFFERINGS OF FARM ANIMALS

What do we think of when we stroll along the aisles of the supermarket looking at the almost clinical cellophane-wrapped parcels of lamb or beef? Few of us have had the opportunity to see what goes on in the production of meat. Our ideas about farming are often based on childhood picture-book illustrations of happy cows, fluffy yellow chicks, and pink pigs with curly tails running around a farmyard. Our ideas about farming – if we have any – can be highly romanticized and sanitized. Most of us have never set foot in a farmyard, and I probably wouldn't have either, if it were not for the fact that I'd trained as a vet. I'd like to take you on a guided tour of the modern farm. We don't have the time or space to look at every detail, or every animal; I will give just a few examples to convey a feeling for what life is like for a farm animal today.

Life for farm animals nowadays is not pleasant and you will almost certainly find parts of this account distressing. The accounts I give are of general modern farm practices – they don't represent the worst (and sometimes illegal) things that go on in the factory farm. There are relatively compassionate farmers who keep their animals in far better conditions than I describe. In addition, the regulations governing animal welfare, as well as the degree of enforcement of those regulations, varies from country to country. In some ways animals in less industrialized countries have freer lives, but in other ways life – and death – for animals, just as for humans, can be far crueller in poorer parts of the world. What you are about to read is a fairly typical account of how farm animals live in the industrialized world.

Cattle
A cow's natural life expectancy is twenty years – fairly long for an animal – but most won't live beyond four. The demands placed upon their bodies, draining milk at a rate which nature never intended, will typically leave them spent by their fourth year. Naturally, their bodies would produce less than 1,000 litres of milk in a year. Due to selective breeding and modern husbandry techniques, they deliver between 6,000 and 12,000 litres.

To achieve this they are milked almost all year round, even while pregnant. There is a period of only a few weeks during which they are given a respite. This is when they are heavily pregnant and their body simply couldn't cope with a growing foetus as well as milking.

Dairy cows often experience metabolic diseases because they can't take in enough nutrition to meet the demands of the milking machine. Their systems may run short of calcium or magnesium, bringing them to the point where they physically collapse. The demands placed on the cows' metabolism mean that they are often effectively malnourished, no matter how much they eat.

Cows are commonly artificially inseminated with semen from one of the large beef breeds. This gives a more valuable calf, which is good for the farmer. Unfortunately for the cow, this means that they give birth to a far larger calf than their pelvic girdle allows for. They frequently suffer greatly giving birth to these huge offspring, or require Caesarean operations, which weaken them further and shorten their lives.

A cow has to calve every year to produce milk, but her calf is taken away shortly after birth and fed on reconstituted milk. The mother's milk is too valuable a commodity to waste on a calf. Like most animals, the cow has a strongly developed maternal instinct and it's distressing for her to lose her calf. It's upsetting for the calf as well.

Whereas a calf would have suckled, on and off, all day long, the cow is milked by machine, usually only twice a day. Cows frequently suffer from painful mastitis – due mainly to the amount of milk they have to produce. The pressure of accumulated milk causes great pain. Cows sometimes kick their own udders because they are in such distress. Eventually the strain may cause the ligaments of the udder to give way and the cow will be useless for milking. A short trip to the abattoir and her brief life is over.

People often assume that cows produce milk just because they are cows, and that producing milk is what they do – as if it were their job. But cows produce milk only in order to feed a calf. They have to be made pregnant every year so that they keep producing milk. This results in a lot of calves as a side-effect of milk production. What happens to a calf once it is taken from its mother? Not many need to be kept to maintain the dairy herd. Some 42 per cent of them end up as beef at around eighteen months old. Some are sent off a few days old to be reared as veal. The meat industry and the dairy industry are inseparable and as much as 80 per cent of beef comes from dairy farms.

The calves destined to become beef tend to have the most natural lives. Some are kept on grass and can roam relatively freely, although many live out their lives on concrete and are fed concentrates to accelerate their growth. They may be castrated and dehorned. Both these operations are highly stressful and usually very painful. The animals find being handled very distressing and they are often castrated without anaesthetic. Animals are dehorned to make them safer to handle. The operation should be performed under local anaesthetic. Unfortunately, animals are usually dehorned in batches, so the anaesthetic often hasn't started to work or it may have begun to wear off by the time the dehorning starts. Worse still, I knew one vet who didn't always use anaesthetics at all because some farmers wouldn't pay the extra cost. 'If they see me taking the anaesthetic out of my bag they just laugh,' he told me.

You may wonder why having a horn cut off requires anaesthetics. The reason is that horns contain nerves and blood vessels. Having a horn removed is not like having your fingernails trimmed but more like having a finger or even a hand sawn off.

Veal was originally just the meat of an unweaned one- or two-day-old calf. Because they were so young, and had never eaten grass or exercised, their meat was unusually pale and tender. It was also expensive because there isn't much eating on a baby calf. Now veal production has become an industrial process. The calves are still taken from their mothers at a day old, but they are now kept in highly artificial conditions in order to keep their flesh pale and soft. Veal calves often live in pens so small that they can barely move. This stops them from using their muscles, so their flesh remains very tender. Sometimes they are kept in virtual darkness because there is a rather irrational belief that this contributes to the paleness of the meat. This makes observation for illness next to impossible, of course, so disease may go untreated.

However, the very nature of veal production prevents the welfare of veal calves being of crucial interest to those who rear them. The calves are allowed no solid food and are fed only on milk substitutes deficient in iron. Veal calves are *deliberately* made ill with anaemia in order to keep the meat pale. A malnourished calf is the whole point of the veal system. In addition, their stomachs, which are designed to process large quantities of roughage, are deprived of anything solid whatsoever. The calves are not even allowed straw to lie on in case they eat it. Their craving for roughage is so strong that they chew on wood and eat their own coats. Their lives are very distressing.

However, even before the calves reach the veal units they have to face the stresses of transportation. It's unpleasant and distressing for us to be in a bus or crowded underground train in the rush-hour; how much more so then for animals being transported for (as current UK regulations allow) up to 28 hours in such conditions, for much of that time unable to feed or drink. At least when we endure such circumstances for a much shorter period we know why we are there – the animals are terror-stricken because of the unfamiliarity of the whole experience. It was against these movements of animals that thousands of people protested at airports and docks in the UK in 1995. These mass demonstrations resulted in changes in the regulations affecting UK veal production, but conditions in many other parts of the world are unchanged.

Chickens
Chickens are reared in more intensive conditions than any other farm animal. Despite the increased availability of so-called free-range eggs the overwhelming majority of laying chickens still live in tiny wire cages in vast sheds. Usually there are five birds to a cage, and each bird has a living space slightly less than the size of this opened book. There is hardly enough room to turn

round. Birds kept in these conditions develop 'vices', or destructive behavioural habits, and they often have their beaks painfully severed to prevent them from pecking at, and even eating, each other. It's worth adding that chickens are not particularly nasty creatures. It's simply intensely frustrating for them not to be able to fulfil any of their natural urges. They aren't able to stretch their wings, dust-bathe, walk, establish social structures, forage for food, or sit on eggs. Take away these natural outlets and birds go mad.

The wire of the cages imprisoning the birds irritates their feet, resulting in sores that will go untreated (with 30,000 birds in a shed there is no personal attention). The birds' feet can even become 'welded' to the wire mesh as their claws or flesh grow around the metal. If they are lucky they are within reach of food and water when this happens.

Laying birds are usually killed at the end of a year. They are all females, of course. Skilled workers separate the males from the females at one day old and treat them as a waste product. They may be killed by gassing, or suffocated in rubbish bags, or they may be thrown into boxes where they crush and suffocate each other. Some, it is claimed, are thrown live into mincing machines to be used for animal feed.[1] They look exactly like the fluffy yellow Easter chicks that we see on greetings cards.

Many so-called free-range chickens don't fare much better. Despite the more attractive label, many rarely get outside. They are often crammed into sheds in their tens of thousands in conditions that are far from natural.

These overcrowded conditions also prevent the birds from fulfilling their full range of natural activities and from establishing a proper social structure. Bullying and stress are common. A small group of dominant and aggressive hens can prevent the others from getting to the outside world, making a nonsense of the 'free-range' label.

Chickens for eating are called 'broilers.' They live (you're probably getting the hang of this by now) in huge sheds in tens of thousands, sometimes crowded together on the floor in a living carpet, sometimes in racks of cages. The amount of space recommended by the Ministry of Agriculture gives them about the same amount of room, when fully grown, as a battery hen.

They stand on their own accumulated faeces, which quickly become disease-ridden. The lights are dimmed to reduce the stress of overcrowding so the stockman probably won't see animals that are ill or have died. In any event there may be only one stockman for tens of thousands of birds, making effective supervision impossible. Health experts consider these sheds to be a serious hazard for workers. As one writer points out:

> Researchers warned chicken farmers to spend as little time as possible in their sheds and to wear a respirator when they go in. But the study said nothing about respirators for the chickens.[2]

Pigs

Few pigs will ever have the opportunity to be outside, to run, to wallow in mud, to dig, to nest (yes, wild pigs build nests), or to play. Pigs are as smart as clever dogs, and like most intelligent animals pigs are very playful.

Instead, most pigs live in concrete boxes or are confined by iron bars in warehouse-sized sheds. The breeding sows have the worst time of it. Most of the time they stand singly in stalls so narrow that they are unable to turn round. They have no bedding and lie on bare concrete. Pigs don't find it any easier than you or I to lie on concrete, so you can perhaps imagine the discomfort. They have no way of socializing or playing or of fulfilling any of their natural impulses. Life is brutally painful and devastatingly boring.

The sow leaves her stall only when it is time for mating or for transfer to the farrowing accommodation where she will give birth to her litter. Again she lives on bare concrete and often can do nothing except lie down and stand up because the space is too narrow to allow anything else.

A farm worker snaps her piglets' eye-teeth off, severs their tails, and castrates the males – all usually at a few days old and without anaesthetic. After weaning, the piglets are kept in batches – usually on a concrete slatted floor in a bare concrete box. Any intelligent animal would become bored in such conditions and pigs are no exception. They often become so frustrated in such unnatural and limiting conditions that they become deranged. Young pigs often indulge in neurotic behaviour such as suckling each other or inanimate objects. They frequently go insane. A common sign of this is tail-biting, where pigs bite the tails of their fellow-inmates, gnawing them to the base of the spine. This is why they have their tails removed at an early age. However, once bored pigs have reached this level of psychopathy they may gnaw the remaining stump of the tail as far down as they can. Another similar 'vice' that pigs develop in these conditions is vulva-biting. The prominent vulva of the females is an easy target for a deranged pig.

Because so many pigs live in one building, airborne infections spread easily. As a result, pneumonia is widespread. When animals stand on slats above their own faeces and urine, as they usually do, the ammonia produced is an irritant to the respiratory system, further aiding the spread of respiratory infections. Leg injuries and arthritis are common because the pigs live on concrete and cannot exercise, and because forced rapid growth puts strain on the joints.

The concrete boxes in which fattening pigs live commonly overheat in warm weather. Since pigs, contrary to the popular saying, cannot sweat, they have to roll in their own faeces to keep cool. Imagine yourself in the same position.

If you are beginning to think that pigs are nasty animals because of tail- and vulva-biting then think again. You won't see this kind of behaviour in the wild. It is the result of sheer boredom. They are signs of insanity. Humans kept in similar conditions would do crazy things as well. The 'vice' is surely not that of the animal but the conditions that bring about this derangement.

Sheep

Sheep are the least intensively reared farm animals. In most of the world they tend to have relatively natural lives, brought indoors only for lambing and receiving little handling except during shearing and dipping. The downside of this is that they often die through exposure, neglect, or starvation. Sheep form a large percentage of the 16,000 large animals that die on British farms every day.[3] Many sheep are kept on hill farms and at lambing time in particular their mortality rate, due to disease and exposure to a harsh hill climate, is especially high. In Britain, 23 per cent of single-born lambs and 55 per cent of twins die on extensive pastures.[4]

The thick woolly coats that we associate with sheep are not entirely natural but are the product of selective breeding, or 'unnatural selection'. In the rain their wool soaks up masses of water (making for a fairly miserable sheep), and in the summer they overheat. Sheep are very prone to painfully itchy skin infections due to their woolly coats. The organophosphate chemicals in which they are dipped to prevent the spread of parasitic diseases are a major health hazard for the farmers, who don't actually have to go into the dip-bath. What does it do to the sheep?

A sheep's main problem is its lack of financial value. Few sheep are worth much, so they tend not to be given prompt medical attention. If you ever see sheep grazing 'kneeling down' it's because standing is too painful for them. This happens when the ground is persistently wet during periods of heavy rainfall, and fungal infections, followed by secondary bacterial infections, invade the hoofs, causing great pain. Judging by the severity of some of the cases I've observed, first aid for sheep is not usually a priority.

A story one farmer told me sums up the lack of regard given to individual sheep. One of his ewes was having trouble lambing. Rather than waste money calling the vet to do a Caesarean – which would cost as much as the ewe was worth – he did the operation himself, with a carving knife and no anaesthetic. He was pleased with himself for having saved money.

The kind of treatment farm animals receive may seem incredible. What would happen if you or I tried to keep a dog in the conditions that a pig has to endure, or if we confined a pet bird so that it couldn't spread its wings? In any civilized country a court would quite rightly prosecute us for cruelty. Farmers can keep animals in such conditions only because of the demand for cheap meat. There is a chain of causality connecting a consumer's appetite with the kind of suffering we have seen.

Fish are the only commonly eaten animals living an entirely natural life (except for farmed fish). However, their death through suffocation when they are taken from the water must be deeply unpleasant. Fish farming causes serious pollution, not least because of the heavy metals used in anti-fouling paints used to prevent molluscs and seaweed colonizing the fishes' cages. We have to remember that eating fish also puts us into competition with fish-eating wildlife. Part of the true price of fish is the culling programmes carried out on wild animals like seals and birds of prey to make sure there are enough fish for human consumption. Vast numbers of the fish caught in nets are not used for human consumption. The fishing industry call them 'trash', and dumps their corpses at sea. 'Trash' can constitute as much as half of a catch.[5] An additional indicator of our lack of regard for both fish and land animals is that 40 to 50 per cent of the world's fish catch is fed to farm animals – most of which are naturally vegetarian.[6]

THE WAY OF ALL FLESH

Neither with their legs nor with their horns do the cows hurt anybody, being obedient like lambs and yielding jars of milk. The king, seizing them by the horns, had them killed by a sword.

Then the gods, the ancestors, Indra, the titans and the demons cried out as the sword fell on the cows: 'This is unjust!'[7]

Few of us would wish to visit an abattoir. They are hellish places. The stench of death, the blood-slicked floors, the noise of machinery, chain-saws tearing flesh and bone, the report of the captive bolt pistols that stun animals before they have their throats cut and, above all, the noises of fear and distress as animals are led to their deaths; all contribute to make a slaughterhouse a hell on earth.

In the abattoir, haste is essential to keep costs down. Animals have to be bullied to come forward to the killing area as quickly as possible. Some abattoir workers believe that a distressed animal makes for better meat due to the release of adrenaline. This 'fight or flight' hormone – released in conditions of fear – tenderizes the muscles and helps stop the meat from becoming infected with bacteria. Slaughtermen are often therefore at no pains to make the animals' last minutes less distressing than they need be. Electric cattle prods goad animals towards the slaughtering area. That these implements are distressing can be inferred from the fact that they are a favoured instrument of torture in countries with the worst records of human rights abuses.

Abattoir workers have to stun all animals that are to be slaughtered to lessen the animals' distress. The exception to this is Muslim (halal) or Jewish (kosher) slaughter, where animals are fully conscious while they are turned upside-down and have their throats cut. The distress of this is unimaginable, and it is worth remembering that many animals slaughtered in this way end up on the shelves of our supermarkets.[8]

A common method of stunning is by captive-bolt pistol. A metal rod is fired from a gun into the brain, destroying the higher functions. A flexible plastic rod is then inserted in the bullet hole and stirred to destroy the reflexes in the lower brain – a process known as 'pithing'. Pithing is done to prevent the corpse from thrashing around and injuring the workers. Pigs, and sometimes sheep, are often stunned with electric tongs, which, in theory, render the animal unconscious. More rarely a carbon dioxide gas chamber may be used. These have been described by researchers as causing 'severe respiratory distress'.[9]

Electric tongs are, understandably, dangerous to the workers, and problems arise because low voltages are used in order to render them less hazardous. Animals commonly begin to recover consciousness before they are killed. In any event some people believe that animals stunned in this way are not unconscious at all, merely paralysed. One hopes that this is not true – it must be appalling to be aware of what is happening but unable even to cry out. Even when carried out effectively the electric stunning is likely to be extremely painful, as humans who have experienced similar shocks report.[10] The actual killing is achieved by cutting the arteries that carry blood to the brain.

Chickens are killed in specialized processing plants. They too have to be stunned first, and this is usually done by suspending them upside-down by the legs on a conveyor line that leads them towards an electrically charged saline bath. Inevitably, as some of the birds struggle, they manage to miss being stunned and are still conscious when they reach the rotating blades that sever the carotid arteries.

Some authorities believe it is better to allow animals destined for slaughter to see their fellows being killed in order to shorten the time they have to wait in terror. Others hold that animals should wait longer so that they are spared seeing their fellows being killed.[11] It is a useful exercise in empathy to decide which we would prefer if such circumstances were forced upon us. Afterwards we could reflect on whether we want to put animals in that situation at all.

2

WHY ARE WE BEASTLY TO ANIMALS?

If we are beginning to become aware of the suffering involved in the meat trade, but still eat meat, then we have a problem. We have a source of conflict in our lives.

We have to decide what to do with that awareness of the suffering inherent in meat-eating. It's all too tempting to push the awareness away so that we can carry on acting as before. We may even recall having done this in the past with this very issue. Another, and more creative, response would be to face up to and explore the conflict so that we can learn and grow from the insights this might reveal. A good place to begin is with an exploration of the views and assumptions that underlie meat-eating and provide a foundation for the practices of the farm and slaughterhouse.

One of the most powerful insights of Buddhism is that behind every action is a *view*. Views are not necessarily philosophical positions that we have carefully worked out; in fact we may never put some of our deepest-held views into words at all. Our views are more likely to be held as unconscious 'inherited' assumptions about the world. These assumptions guide and give rise to our actions. Bringing views into consciousness, and recognizing where they have come from and how they affect us, is a valuable exercise. It gives us the power to change our views for ones that will bring more harmony and fulfilment to our lives.

Applying this principle to meat-eating, we can see that many of our views about our relations with animals come from the Judeo-Christian model of the world. Even if we don't believe in the biblical account of the world it probably affects us unconsciously. After all, it has shaped the Western psyche for close on two millennia. Some of the views that we have unconsciously absorbed from this tradition stand in the way of our respect and compassion for animals.

Firstly, we have inherited the view that humankind has dominion over the animals and that we therefore have a 'right' to kill animals and that it is 'natural' for them to live in fear of us. We have come to assume that animals have been put on earth for us to use, and that their suffering is unimportant if it arises as a result of our use of them.

> Let us make man in our image, after our likeness: and let them have dominion over the fish of the sea, and over the fowl of the air, and over the cattle, and over all the earth, and over every creeping thing that creepeth upon the earth.[12]

The book of Genesis clarifies what this stewardship entails when God tells Noah:

> And the fear of you and the dread of you shall be upon
> every beast of the earth, and upon every fowl of the air,
> upon all that moveth upon the earth, and upon all the
> fishes of the sea; into your hand are they delivered.
> Every moving thing that liveth shall be meat for you.[13]

Consequently, most of us believe that 'Thou shalt not kill' does not apply to animals. The Western approach has typically been to see a rigid separation between humans and animals, with humans having a 'soul' or 'rationality' setting us apart. Westerners have generally seen human suffering as a matter for concern (with some important exceptions) while we have tended to ignore or deny animal suffering much of the time.

This view of animals as possessions to be used in any way we please became a philosophical standpoint for many Western thinkers. Thomas Aquinas, probably the greatest medieval European philosopher, wrote:

> We cannot wish good things to an irrational creature,
> because it is not competent, properly speaking, to
> possess good.... Nevertheless we can love irrational
> creatures out of charity, if we regard them as the good
> things that we desire for others.[14]

In other words we can only care for the welfare of animals if it will benefit a human, not for the sake of the animal.

The philosopher Descartes and his disciples developed yet further the idea that, because they are 'irrational', we can treat animals in any way we wish. Descartes regarded animals as no more than complex mechanisms, devoid of rationality. His followers took this line of reasoning to its logical conclusion. If an animal has no 'soul', and is merely a mechanism, then the cries of an animal when it is injured no more signify that it is in pain than the rattling of a faulty engine suggests that an automobile suffers. His followers 'kicked about their dogs and dissected their cats without mercy, laughing at any compassion for them, and calling their screams the noise of breaking machinery', according to one of his biographers.[15]

This was probably the low point of Western relations with animals (although some factory farming methods come close), but some people have expressed such views well into the twentieth century. In the 1960s a theologian claimed that animals exhibit 'a very interesting and, indeed, very mysterious psychism, but one that is *devoid of consciousness of any kind*'. (Original emphasis retained.) He goes on to conclude that

the problem of animal 'suffering' is an empty one, as 'unconscious suffering' is a contradiction in terms. To suffer and not to be aware of the fact, to suffer and not to be conscious of suffering, is the same as not suffering at all.[16]

One powerfully influential scientific view of the early twentieth century came from the same current of thought. The school of 'behaviourism', whose most famous exponent was B.F. Skinner, dismissed the idea of animals having any self-consciousness. Like Descartes, he saw animals as complex machines devoid of the capacity to experience pain. Although this view has lost ground, it still has its exponents in the scientific community today. As recently as 1992, a serious scientific magazine could carry an article entitled 'Do Animals Feel Pain?'[17] The article reported that a working party of experts rather tentatively decided, after three years of deliberation, that vertebrates (which include all farm animals) '*may* be capable of experiencing *some* suffering'. (My emphasis.)

It would be wrong to suppose that all Christians (or scientists) hold, or have held, the inhumane views we've touched upon. Many have taken a leading role in animal welfare, and some Christians (and scientists) are vegetarian and have a strongly compassionate relationship with the animal world. However, traditional Western views have deeply conditioned many of us and underpin our acceptance of the modern horrors of the factory farm, where animals are treated as machines, and where the pain they feel is regarded as inconsequential.

THE BUDDHIST PERSPECTIVE

At first one should meditate intently on the equality of oneself and others as follows: 'All equally experience suffering and happiness. I should look after them as I do myself.... I should dispel the suffering of others because it is suffering like my own suffering.'[18]

The Buddhist view of animals and their relation to humans is rather different from the traditional Western viewpoint outlined above. Buddhism has always recognized that animals show every sign of experiencing and fearing suffering. That animals lack some faculties that humans have, or have them less well developed, is a separate issue, and not one that affects animals' ability to suffer. Buddhism sees suffering as undesirable and freedom from suffering as something to be preferred, irrespective of whether it is an animal or a human that suffers.

Buddhism, then, regards animals as being worthy of our respect, and urges us to have compassion for animals when we see they are suffering. When they are free from suffering Buddhism also encourages us to respect that fact and not to cause them any unnecessary pain or distress.

In the West, the myth of humans being given dominion over the animals has shaped Western relations with nature. Many Buddhist myths and symbols, recognizing the continuity between animals and humans, and showing that all sentient life is intimately interrelated, are expressive of the Buddhist approach to animals. One such traditional Buddhist symbol is called the Wheel of Life.[19] This shows six realms of existence, including the realm of animals and the human realm.

The Wheel of Life is a symbol of change; it shows us how we progress or regress, depending on how we act. Buddhism does not see the realms as being completely separate from one another – beings can die in one realm and be reborn in another. Animals may be reborn as humans in the future and, possibly, those of us who are humans now may be reborn as animals. There is no absolute discontinuity, in the Buddhist account, between animals and humans. Instead, our continuity and commonality are emphasized. Animals and humans are, so to speak, all trapped on the Wheel, one of whose characteristics is a tendency to suffering.

As well as this symbol, there are many popular folk tales, called Jatakas, about the Buddha's previous lives. In some of these stories – which are similar to Aesop's fables – the Buddha is portrayed as an animal. Usually he is the animals' leader and performs heroic deeds that benefit others.[20] These stories illustrate Buddhist teachings through the simple, direct medium of storytelling rather than doctrinally.

These myths are not presented as reasons for becoming vegetarian, but as an illustration of how fundamentally different the Buddhist view of animals is from the Western view. Although there is no need for Western Buddhists to believe that the Buddha was literally an animal in previous lives, we can learn from the Jataka tales that early Buddhists had no problem with thinking about their revered teacher as having been an animal in a past life.[21] Once more, animals and humans are seen as part of a continuum of life.

Although humans may or may not literally be reborn as animals, the underlying message of these images – that there is similarity and continuity between animals and humans – is something we can learn from. We all have the capacity to suffer and the desire to escape suffering. There is therefore no question of Buddhists regarding animals as 'things', to be possessed or treated as if they were objects without feelings. There is also no question of animals having been put here for us to use. Instead, we're all trapped in this Wheel of Life together. The main difference between humans and animals is that humans have a greater ability to seek and create happiness – for ourselves and others. Buddhism encourages us to empathize with animals and see them as worthy of our kindness and compassion.

3

BUDDHIST ETHICS

NON-HARM

There's a story from China, telling of the meeting between a provincial governor and a Buddhist teacher. In
search of profound teachings, the governor risked his
life going into the wild mountains where the sage, Tao-
lin, lived. The governor must have been sorely disap-
pointed when Tao-lin summed up the essence of
Buddhism in the words 'Cease to do evil; learn to do
good.'

'Even a three-year-old child can understand that,' said
the puzzled, and perhaps even contemptuous, official.

'That's true,' said Tao-lin, 'A child of three can understand it, but a grown-up of eighty finds it difficult to
practise.'[22]

Not everything that sounds simple *is* simple. The
Buddha often spoke in a very simple, direct way, as in
the following from the *Dhammapada*:

> All beings tremble before danger, all fear death. When a
> man considers this, he does not kill or cause to kill.
>
> All beings fear before danger, life is dear to all. When
> a man considers this, he does not kill or cause to kill.[23]

These words are easy to understand – on the surface. But behind the simplicity of these verses lies a deep and radically transforming vision of existence.

We can do no greater harm than to kill another sentient being. Killing is the ultimate expression of indifference to the well-being of others. All, except in the most extreme circumstances, cherish life. In the contemporary hell of the modern slaughterhouse animals cry out and cower in terror when they realize that their life is nearing a premature end. All beings, except in the most desperate circumstances, try to escape death.

We often wish to deny the inescapable fact that meat-eating requires killing to take place. In order for meat to appear on a plate an animal must die. Our appetites are part of a complex chain of events resulting in suffering and death. Meat-eating inevitably entails the violence of the slaughterhouse and farm. Most of us have been brought up eating meat and we have not been encouraged to think much about this. And few of us will have seen farm animals suffering. If we actually saw an animal in terror in front of us, about to be killed, we might feel compassion and wish the animal to go free, but the 'nasty business' is usually conveniently hidden away.

Few people are aware what happens to animals reared for slaughter, or what death in an abattoir is like. Few of us have had any real contact with farms other than seeing animals grazing in the fields as we travel past. This isn't surprising. Much of what happens on modern farms – as we've seen – is deeply unpleasant. Because of this farmers tend to be defensive and even secretive about what they do.[24] A friend of mine who was involved in making documentary films told me she found it easier to get access to nuclear power stations than to farms.

Often it is a question of 'out of sight, out of mind.' We don't know and, frankly, we'd often rather not know, what goes on in order to feed us. We'd rather not feel connected with the results of our actions. We'd rather perpetuate our alienation – our lack of a sense of connectedness with other living beings, because, of course, 'knowing' and 'connecting' bring uncomfortable pressures to bear in our lives.

But now, perhaps, we have more awareness of the consequences of our actions when we eat meat. When we are more aware that our appetites can lead to real suffering we may even feel an urge to change. That urge may be strong enough to make us give up meat at once – for ever. On the other hand we may just have a niggling doubt and find ourselves with an uneasy conscience.

For many of us, eating meat is very pleasurable, and changing our diet may be a sacrifice we are reluctant to make. However, once we are truly aware of the consequences of our actions, we are in a dilemma. Our deeper, more ethical response is one of compassion for the animals that are harmed in order for us to have meat. This sense of compassion is in conflict with our habits and our desire to keep on doing what seems pleasurable.

In dilemmas of this sort I find the only effective remedy is to go to the root of the problem and sort out on an ethical level the conflict that exists between my actions and my conscience. I need to remove the source of ethical discomfort by deciding to give up actions that cause harm and by following through that resolution as best as I can. Once I have decided to align myself with what is best within me and act in accord with it I find that my life changes for the better. When, after my visit to an abattoir, I decided to become a vegetarian, my attachment to eating meat started to wither away very quickly. Many other people have had the same experience. We find that our tastes change and that meat stops looking attractive and starts to look distasteful. We'll find that our friends begin to respect us for having taken an ethical stance – although one or two may be unsure at first. We may even find that we become more confident having taken a decision that is courageous, going as it does against the norms of our culture. Giving up meat can prove to be a positive relief.

INTERCONNECTEDNESS AND METTA

Underlying the verses from the *Dhammapada* is the Buddha's observation that nothing exists in isolation. If we attempted to sum up in one word the Buddha's vision of reality, perhaps the best we could use is 'interconnectedness'. We exist only in relation to the world, as part of a web of interconnectedness. It's impossible for us to be truly happy without recognizing the fact of this interconnectedness and, just as importantly, changing the way that we relate to the world.

At first reading, this may seem counter-intuitive. After all, you're sitting reading this book. You know where 'you' end and where 'the rest of the world' begins. Outside the window are other people, with other lives. The nearest farm may be miles away. And here you are, with your life. Why can't we just 'look after number one' and learn to be happy without considering others? It might seem obvious that we're independent.

But reflect a moment. How independent are we? Physically you may see 'yourself' ending where the air touches your skin. But that same air is also nourishing your body. Try holding your breath and see how long you can maintain your independence. The experiment can't last long. The air that was 'out there', and 'other' is now an intimate part of 'you', and the air that you exhale was, moments ago, part of your muscles and tissues. When did it stop being 'you' exactly? The body that is doing this breathing is made up of food that grew all over the world. It was once soil, and air, and sunshine, and rainwater, and manure, and plants, and animals. The food only became part of you because of an immense number of people – those who planted crops, those who transported them, and the people who brought up, cared for, educated, and gave medicine to those people. An uncountable number of people were involved in making the body that is holding this book. You could not have existed without them. So how independent are we, really? The answer is not at all, physically.

But what about the level of our personality? (If we've realized that our physical 'self' exists only in interdependence then perhaps we can still, for the moment, assume that some other part of ourselves does not.) What about our minds? Can you imagine your mind without language? Where would 'you' be without it? Where did your language come from? You learned it from other people, of course. Even the concepts you use have been picked up from the world around you. Our mind is like a semi-permeable membrane bubble floating on an ocean of ideas. What is inside us was once outside – or, more accurately, what is inside us has arisen in dependence upon what is outside us. Our mind certainly isn't independent.

What about emotionally? Imagine for a moment you've been put in solitary confinement, with no human contact whatsoever – not even through the medium of books. How easy would it be to maintain any level of happiness, even for a few days? Now imagine the door swings open and there are those you love most, come to take you away. How do you feel now? Where is your independence? It's an illusion; one that we need to dispel by waking up – awakening to the reality of our interdependence with the rest of the world. The Buddhist term for this is *pratitya-samutpada*, or 'conditioned co-production', although it could even be translated as 'interdependent existence'. This is the notion – more accurately, the observation – that all things exist only in relationship and not in isolation. *Pratitya-samutpada* has been described as the central teaching of Buddhism – the teaching from which all other teachings flow.

Bearing in mind the total state of interconnectedness in which we exist we have to ask ourselves whether it is possible for us to be truly happy without taking that into account. The answer, according to Buddhism, is that we cannot. We *are* our relationships. There is no part of us which does not exist in relation to the so-called outside world and to so-called others. If there is disharmony in our relations with others, we will experience dishar-mony in our lives; we will experience the jarring results of conflict. The only way in which we can live at a deeper level of happiness and fulfilment is to change our rela-tionship to the world, so that we experience the results of harmony rather than disharmony.

Although we can't ask them, it seems fair to assume that animals don't want to be eaten. They run away from danger, fight if cornered, and try to escape pain. Let's say we're now aware of that – but let's say we also still desire to eat meat. Emotionally there is likely to be a conflict. Once our awareness has extended to empathy – an emo-tional interconnectedness – the well-being of others is something it is hard to ignore without causing ourselves distress.

Is ignorance bliss? If we remain unaware of the suffer-ing we cause then will we escape the consequences of our actions? According to Buddhism we will not. We can still feel unconscious guilt. 'Very often the unconscious mind is wiser than the conscious mind,' as Sangha-rakshita has said.[25] Witness the defensiveness, and even aggressiveness, some meat-eaters can demonstrate when they encounter a vegetarian. Once we are empathetically aware that animals desire life and freedom from suffering (and maybe contentment, if not happiness) then the most creative way to remove conflict from our lives is to stop causing harm and to encourage the development of empathic feeling.

An empathic feeling which is in support of, rather than in conflict with, another's desire for happiness is what we call *metta*. *Metta* is often translated as 'loving-kindness', or 'universal friendliness', or simply as 'love'. Metta is a cherishing emotion that desires the happiness and well-being of others and wishes that others do not suffer. It's the emotional equivalent of the experience of interconnectedness. This does not of course mean that we can't be happy unless everyone else in the world is happy. However, as long as our attitudes to others are out of harmony with their desire to be happy, we are not going to be truly happy ourselves.

If we want to be happy, what we have to change is not simply 'ourselves' but *the way we relate*. If we want a happy and satisfying life, we need to create more satisfactory ways of relating. Metta is the most harmonious and satisfying way that we can relate to others. Since metta is the desire that others be happy, and since the desire for happiness is universal, metta brings us into deeper harmony with the universe.

We all experience interconnectedness – and metta – to some extent. Interconnectedness is not just some theoretical reflection: it's part of our experience. One example we're all familiar with is empathizing with someone who is upset. If we can understand their world, their pain to some extent becomes our pain and we find we have a desire to alleviate their suffering. We experience what Buddhism calls *karuna*, or compassion. Our ability to do this is part of what makes us truly human. In some mysterious way we seem to be able to explore the emotional landscape of other beings.

This might seem paradoxical – that in talking about how a greater awareness of the well-being of others can help us be happier we're also talking about sharing their discomfort. Over and over, I find to my surprise – and I'm sure you can confirm this from your own experience – that when I am empathizing with someone else's pain I feel close to them and somehow more alive and fulfilled. To deeply experience our connectedness with others seems to be more real than to remain in a false sense of barren isolation.

This sharing of the world of others doesn't only apply to painful experiences, of course. If we're aware that someone else is happy, we often share in their joy, sometimes very intensely. We call this *mudita* or sympathetic joy. Both karuna and mudita are themselves facets of metta. When our metta meets suffering it transmutes into compassion, and when it meets good fortune and happiness in others it manifests as sympathetic joy.

Buddhism sees metta as the fundamental positive emotion. Like any emotion we can experience it in milder as well as in stronger forms. At its strongest it is a passionate and overwhelming desire for the happiness and welfare of all – including animals. In its milder forms it is the patience, care, and kindness we feel towards our family and friends, when we expect nothing back. Metta is an emotion that we all experience from time to time.

The fact that we experience metta, and its sister emotions karuna and mudita, demonstrates our ability to experience our interconnectedness with others. Metta, karuna, and mudita are our deeper, truer responses to the world – the responses that we feel when we are free from superficial and selfish ways of behaving and feeling. They are the emotional dimension of an awareness of interconnectedness.

The Buddha used this principle of interconnectedness to teach ethics. Once, according to the Buddhist scriptures, the Buddha came across some boys tormenting fish in a pond. The Buddha saw the boys frightening the fish, hitting the water with sticks. His response was very straightforward. 'Do you boys fear pain? Do you dislike pain?' he asked.[26] He was pointing out that they were doing something to another that they would not wish done to themselves. Perhaps the boys had never realized this – sometimes we lack the imagination to know that our actions cause suffering. Or perhaps the boys knew intellectually that they were causing suffering but didn't *feel* it was important. Once we understand that another being's suffering is as real as ours, then something shifts in our feelings and actions. With the arising of empathy we become more ethical in our actions, and without empathy true ethics are not possible.

Supporting this kind of empathic teaching are a number of practices that Buddhists follow in order to cultivate metta and eliminate negative emotions. Selfish and limiting emotions are like veils that prevent us from seeing reality. Sometimes we need help to cut through these veils and to cultivate a healthy and positive sense of connectedness. But how do we do this?

ETHICS, MEDITATION, AND INSIGHT

The Buddhist path, in one of its simplest formulations, consists of three aspects of training: ethics, meditation, and insight.[27] These are three areas in which we can train ourselves in order to deepen our awareness of interrelatedness. These practices help us to get rid of selfish emotions that limit our awareness, help us develop the positive emotions that are the emotional experience of interrelatedness, and help us change the way we see the world, so that we come to experience ourselves as part of the fabric of the universe, and not something separate from it.

The Buddhist approach to ethics emphasizes that we need to take responsibility for our actions. Actions form a crucial aspect of our interrelatedness with the world. Buddhist ethics involves seeing that our actions have consequences, either directly or indirectly, for ourselves and for others. Even the indirect effects of our actions are of concern to us within the network of cause and effect of which we are an inseparable part. We might recall that the *Dhammapada* reminds us that when we are in touch with our interconnectedness we do not 'cause to kill' – we do not get others to do our dirty work for us. One aspect of ethical practice involves voluntarily undertaking to follow precepts to guide our actions. There are a number of these, but the most important is that which encourages us to avoid causing harm and to practise metta:

> I undertake the training principle of abstention from causing harm to living beings.
> With deeds of loving-kindness, I purify my body.[28]

When we attempt to follow this precept we are trying to relate to the world on the basis of love rather than on the basis of our desire to gratify our appetites. We try to enter into a deeper realization of our relatedness with other sentient beings and to minimize the harm we cause. We often fail, of course. In fact most of the time we are making mistakes, and we hurt others through deed and word, action and inaction – often without realizing it. But we try to learn from those mistakes, to recognize when we have wandered from the path, and to reorientate ourselves, patiently and kindly, towards our ideals.

We must all have examples of when we were not able to respond compassionately to someone in distress and the shame or guilt we feel when we've let someone down. In not considering someone else's well-being we undermine our own. I notice this most strongly in regard to humans, which is quite natural. After all, it's easier to empathize with a person than it is with an animal – we have many more experiences in common, and can articulate those experiences using language. But from my own experience I know that it applies to animals too. One relatively minor example that springs to mind involves the earthworms that find their way onto a pavement after it has been raining. I used to notice them wriggling around on the concrete, knowing they would likely die as the rain dried up. After some inner struggle I decided to make a point of lifting them on to grass or soil where they stood a better change of surviving. I have to confess to a certain amount of squeamishness regarding earthworms. On the whole though I felt better, having helped even a relatively low form of life, than I did trying to shut out the awareness of their suffering.

Denying our natural ability to experience love and compassion carries a price tag. The next verse of the *Dhammapada* says:

> He who for the sake of their own pleasure, hurts others
> who want happiness, shall not hereafter find
> happiness.[29]

Denying the reality of our interconnectedness with other sentient beings leads to an impoverishment, and even a poisoning, of our own lives. It is an impoverishment, because love or metta is the single most enriching experience we can have. We are most truly fulfilled when we experience metta, and we deny ourselves the richness of this experience when we act without regard for the well-being of others.

Harming other beings results in a poisoning of our lives because the moral unease we feel when we put our own desires above the welfare of others leads to guilt and conflict. When I act callously towards others it creates a tension within my being. On the one hand there is the desire to get what I want, and on the other is a deeper sense of how I should really act – the voice of my conscience. As long as that conflict persists I can never be truly at ease with myself.

In fact, when any of us looks deeply into our present suffering, we will find that much of it can be traced back to a failure to acknowledge interconnectedness – a failure to live ethically. We all live with, and suffer from, the effects of this.

The second aspect of the threefold training is meditation, through which we actively cultivate awareness and metta, and lessen the hold of selfish emotions. Meditation helps us to develop more positive, and more liberating, mental states.[30] We can practise meditations like the 'mindfulness of breathing' which help us to be more aware of ourselves. Often we are not very aware and simply act blindly and habitually. With more awareness we can take more responsibility for our actions and have more choice about whether we want to act ethically or unethically.

Another meditation practice is the 'metta bhavana' – the development of love – which encourages the tendencies we have to feel with – and for – others. In the metta bhavana we aim to cultivate cherishing feelings for all sentient beings – animals included. Metta is part of a group of emotions (also including karuna and mudita, which we've mentioned) called 'the immeasurables', partly because they are the very opposite of the limiting and selfish emotions that prevent us realizing our interconnectedness. Through practising the metta bhavana our sense of self expands until, ultimately, we feel connected with and responsive to all sentient existence.

The third aspect of the threefold training through which we can transform our relationship with the world is the cultivation of Insight. We can learn to see more clearly the reality of interconnectedness. We've already been cultivating this faculty of Insight to some extent, by reading about and reflecting on the subject and by examining the views that underlie our actions. We've also perhaps been stretching our imagination through considering what life is like for farm animals. An awareness of interconnectedness depends on the faculty of imagination, which allows us to put ourselves in someone else's shoes, to see life from their perspective, to share their world. Metta, karuna, and mudita flow naturally from this empathic awareness.

The poet Shelley described this when he said:

> The great secret of morals is love.... A man, to be greatly good, must imagine intensely and comprehensively; he must put himself in the place of another and of many others; the pains and pleasures of his species must become his own.[31]

Of course, we don't always have the intense and comprehensive imagination needed to appreciate the interdependent nature of our lives. As a consequence most of us could not describe ourselves as 'greatly good'. We often push aside a deeper response to the feelings of others, or prevent it from arising. We may find ourselves changing television channels when a programme about world poverty makes us feel uncomfortable. We may wrestle over whether to give a beggar a few coins that we would probably never miss. We may act hurtfully towards someone because we are not happy ourselves or because they have something we want. We behave, in short, as if we *are* separate from others, as if we can find happiness while ignoring the unhappiness of others – even the unhappiness that others experience as a result of our actions. We can develop more Insight by exercising our faculties of imagination and empathy.

Although he refers to the need for us to share the pains and pleasures of our 'species', Shelley himself did not limit his own compassionate outlook to human beings. Shelley was a vegetarian. As mentioned earlier, in some ways it's easier to empathize with humans than with animals. We may have to make a bit more effort to relate to animals in this way; but we do – despite some Western views to the contrary – have a lot in common with animals. In evolutionary terms we are animals ourselves, and fundamentally we share most of the drives, instincts, and emotions of other higher mammals. And our capacity to empathize is vast.

According to Buddhist teachings, we can learn to empathize to such an extent that we no longer see the world in terms of 'self' and 'other'. In this full realization of our interconnectedness we don't act to relieve other beings' suffering in order to make ourselves feel better, but simply because suffering exists, and because those beings desire to be free from it. When we start practising ethics our approach is bound to be somewhat self-referential, but supported by meditation and deep reflection on the nature of reality we can learn to be more truly selfless. Giving up meat and fish – knowing that it will relieve the suffering of living beings – is a simple and practical step that we can all take to help us move towards that ideal.

4

THE BENEFITS OF VEGETARIANISM

Giving up meat means that fewer animals will die, and fewer animals will be reared in the appalling conditions we have looked at. Just by changing your diet you will ensure that there is less suffering in the world. However, the benefits of becoming vegetarian go much further than that. In adopting a vegetarian diet you will have a real impact on the planet in many ways.

We live in a time of unparalleled crisis, with growing environmental problems which some believe may threaten the very existence of our planet. Raising animals for food causes many of those problems, which are therefore avoidable.

Farming animals is intensely wasteful of resources. It has been estimated that 500g of steak from intensively-reared animals consumes 2.5kg of grain, 10,000 litres of water, the energy equivalent of four litres of petrol, and about 16kg of topsoil.[32] Intensive beef production is very wasteful of fossil fuels. In America, intensively-reared beef consumes 33 calories of fossil fuel energy for every calorie of food energy it produces.[33] This short-sighted squandering of the planet's resources is simply not sustainable.

It takes 10kg of plant protein to produce 1kg of animal protein. If a field is capable of producing 10 tonnes of soya beans, we can do two things with it. We can feed humans with the soya beans or we can feed the soya beans to cattle. If we do the latter we effectively lose 90 per cent of the protein and energy value of the original crop, which means we use 10 times more land than is necessary.

Because rearing animals is intrinsically wasteful of land, the demand for ever more farmland has resulted in the loss of more and more of our wilderness areas. We have ripped out hedgerows, felled forests, and drained marshes in order to produce more grazing land for animals. More than 25 per cent of the forests of Central America and 40 million hectares of the Amazon jungle have been cleared for beef production.[34] In the case of the rainforests these natural areas will never recover. Deserts all over the world are expanding as overgrazing leads to depletion of the soil in marginal areas. Our forests produce the very oxygen we breathe, yet we are destroying them in order to make beefburgers.

We are all aware now of the threat of global warming brought about by the build-up of 'greenhouse gases', which trap the sun's warmth in the atmosphere, leading to a rise in global temperatures. We may not be aware that cattle and sheep produce large quantities of methane, which is a greenhouse gas. Farm animals probably produce around 20 per cent of the 400 million tonnes of this gas that is produced every year worldwide.[35] Since global warming may be one of the greatest dangers to the future of our species, a reduction in the numbers of farm animals will help reduce that threat.

Farming animals also produces large amounts of sewage which frequently contaminates aquatic environments.[36] The raised level of nutrients in the water leads to the rapid growth of algae and the death of fish.[37] The pollution of lakes and rivers can have devastating effects, harming human health and livelihoods and impoverishing our environment.

With fewer people eating meat these pressures will lessen and the effects may even be reversed. With more of the population becoming vegetarian we may be able to allow land presently under cultivation to return to wilderness – with more forests, swamps, and moorlands for future generations to thank us for. With more farmland being freed up there is enormous potential for cultivating biomass fuels – plants grown for fuel – which make a zero net contribution to global warming. By adopting a vegetarian diet we will help support a more sustainable world for future generations.

However, perhaps the most worrying side-effect of agricultural activity on humans is the emergence of new disease-causing organisms. According to one authority,

> by far the most potentially destructive effect … is the
> evolution of pathogens with mass destruction potential

when they are transferred to their final host: man. This could produce epidemics paralleled only by the plagues associated with the increase in the population density in the Middle Ages and Victorian epochs.[38]

It's worth contemplating that the medieval plagues wiped out between a third and a half of the population of Europe. The unidentified pathogen that causes BSE in animals and Creutzfeldt-Jakob disease in humans is only one of the latest of these diseases – and we don't yet know how extensive that problem is. Some animal viruses and bacteria have the potential to cross into the human population and this is believed to happen on farms. Cholera, which has killed millions, spread to the human population from sheep and cattle as have many other diseases.[39] The various waves of influenza that periodically sweep the world, causing millions of deaths, are believed to have their origins in agriculture. 20,000,000 people were killed by the influenza epidemic that followed the first World War – 10,000,000 more than died in the war itself.[40]

In late 1997 and early 1998, the entire chicken population of Hong Kong, followed by much of the domestic animal population, had to be exterminated to prevent the spread of a deadly avian virus that had begun to infect humans. A plague may have been averted – but at a tremendous cost in suffering. In early 1999, an outbreak of a deadly strain of encephalitis began in Malaysia, spreading to humans from pigs. At the time of writing, 67 people had died and another 99 had been admitted to hospital. Malaysian farmers are slaughtering hundreds of thousands of pigs to try to prevent a deadly human epidemic.[41] With pig population densities in some parts of Europe reaching 9,000 animals per square kilometre, the potential for a disastrous human epidemic is vast.[42] By lessening our dependence on the growing of animals for food we will be helping to protect the human population, particularly the young and elderly, from such diseases.

Antibiotics are used on animals to treat disease (often arising from the intensive manner in which they are confined) and as a routine food additive to promote faster growth. A UK National Consumer Council report points out that 'some antibiotic residues in food may be toxic and cause some people to become hypersensitive to antibiotics. They could also make bacteria resistant to antibiotics.'[43] The emergence of antibiotic-resistant bacteria is one of the greatest challenges to modern medicine – and much of the problem comes from farming.

The benefits of vegetarianism for our world are far-reaching. Every meal we eat has some say as to which direction our world moves in – towards the ever-accelerating degradation of the planet or towards increasing harmony with nature and a sustainable future for the planet and for our species. These choices are, truly, on our menu. Which will we have?

BENEFITS FOR OUR HEALTH

It certainly isn't necessary to be a vegetarian to be healthy, although I am personally convinced that vegetarianism is, generally speaking, a healthier alternative than meat-eating. And it does seem to be the case that vegetarians are, overall, healthier than average. A paper by the British Nutrition Foundation says that 'many studies have shown that vegetarians as a group have lower rates of heart disease and of some cancers, and may also benefit from the reduced risk of some other conditions'.[44] A massive study of over 120,000 men in Japan showed that simply adding meat to the diet increased the risk of dying from heart disease by 30 per cent.[45] A recent UK government report recommended that those eating an average 90g of meat (less than a quarter-pound hamburger) per day should consider cutting back.[46]

There are, of course, good and bad vegetarian diets and whatever diet one follows it is important to eat healthily. If we eat a varied and interesting vegetarian diet there is little or no risk of deficiencies, and a good prospect of living a longer and more healthy life. The chart on page 56 gives an example of the food sources that can form the basis of a healthy vegetarian diet.

Ultimately, I am attempting to convert people to vegetarianism not on health grounds, but on ethical grounds. However, a point that we often need to highlight is that vegetarianism is a perfectly healthy option. Many people still have worries that a vegetarian diet might not be healthy, though in fact becoming vegetarian is one of the simplest steps they could take to improve their chance of a long and healthy life. Below I outline the main nutritional issues that can arise for someone switching to a vegetarian diet.

GROUP	PROVIDES	EXAMPLES	SERVING
Whole grains and potatoes	Energy, protein, essential oils, vitamins, dietary fibre	Whole grains are the most nutritious: bread, flour, pasta, rice, cous-cous, bulgar, millet, potatoes, etc.	1–2 portions per meal
Nuts and legumes	Protein, oils, fibre	Chickpeas, lentils, nuts, soya products (tofu, tempeh, TVP, etc.), saitan, peanuts, nut butters, tahini, sesame and sunflower seeds, etc.	2 portions daily. Combine these foods with each other and with those in the group above
Green and orange vegetables	Vitamins, minerals, protein	Broccoli, spinach, kale, spring greens, brussels sprouts, water-cress, carrots, dried apricots, yams, sweet potatoes, etc.	1–2 portions per meal
Fruit	Energy, vitamins, minerals	All kinds, including fruit and vegetable juices	Daily
Fats and oils	Energy, essential oils	Preferably olive and sunflower oils, margarines (preferably fortified with B_{12})	Use sparingly
Other	Vitamin and trace minerals	For iron: wholegrain cereals, wholemeal bread, dark green vegetables, pulses, nuts, dried fruit, molasses or treacle.	Some of these with every meal
		For B_{12}: for vegans and pregnant or lactating women in particular: B_{12} tablets, fortified soya milk, vegetable stock, yeast extracts, some margarines	Daily

Some will say that it's natural for us to eat meat. I often wonder if they have thought through the idea of meat-eating being natural. For example, when a lion takes control of a pride his first action is to kill all the offspring of the previous dominant male so that his own offspring will have the best chance of surviving. This is natural, but we would hardly use it as a basis for human morality. That something is natural does not mean it is ethical. Humans are capable of living in ways that transcend 'animal' nature and, from an ethical point of view, it is only by so doing that we can become truly human.

In a very real sense meat-eating is not natural for us: we are poorly adapted to eating meat. The human gut is proportionately far longer than that of a carnivore, and this is probably why meat-eaters have a far higher incidence of bowel cancer than vegetarians. A likely explanation is that the bacterial breakdown of meat in the gut produces carcinogenic by-products. True carnivores, like cats and dogs, have a much shorter length of gut in proportion to their body than us, and can expel waste more quickly. We just don't seem to be cut out to eat flesh. You could say that it just isn't natural for us to eat meat.

Our bodies are also not good at dealing with the amount of fat found in meat. The editor of the *American Journal of Cardiology* wrote that 'no matter how much fat carnivores eat, they do not develop atherosclerosis'.[47] He went on to say that dogs, even when fed a massive 200 times the average level of cholesterol that Americans ingest, do not develop heart disease.[48] Heart disease in humans is, of course, a major killer.

People often have worries about iron, calcium, and protein, and fear that these are deficient in a vegetarian diet. None of these concerns has any real basis in fact. According to the American Dietetic Association, 'appropriately planned vegetarian diets are healthful, are nutritionally adequate, and provide health benefits in the prevention and treatment of certain diseases.'[49] Let's take a look at these specific nutrients.

Iron

Many women in particular worry about anaemia, which is, of course, more common in women due to blood loss during menstruation. They have understandable concerns that a vegetarian or vegan diet might make them more likely to suffer from this condition. However, as the British Nutrition Foundation points out, 'studies of haemoglobin levels indicate no significant differences between vegetarian and non-vegetarian groups, or between vegans and controls.'[50] Anaemia seems to be no more of a problem in vegetarians than in meat-eaters, for plants can provide all the iron most healthy people need. Leafy green vegetables, wholemeal bread, molasses, dried fruits, lentils, and pulses are all important sources of iron. For those who are clinically anaemic, whether meat-eaters or vegetarians, it is preferable to take an iron supplement rather than rely solely on dietary iron.

Calcium

Osteoporosis (weakening of the bones) is another disease that affects mainly women, usually in later life, and again many people worry about whether a vegetarian diet can supply enough calcium. This may be rather ironic, since a study in America showed that women on a vegetarian diet had half the chance of developing osteoporosis than women who were omnivorous.[51] Other studies, however, have shown no significant differences between bone density in vegetarian and omnivorous women. At the very least we can say with confidence that a lack of calcium is not a problem for most vegetarians. Perhaps surprisingly, osteoporosis is most common in countries where the population eat a lot of meat and dairy products. It is least common in countries like China and Japan where many people eat a mainly vegetarian or vegan diet.[52]

Important vegetarian sources of calcium are dairy products, leafy green vegetables, bread, nuts, and seeds (especially sesame seeds), dried fruits, calcium supplemented soya milk, and tofu.

Protein

While it's mostly women who have concerns about iron and calcium, it often seems to be men who worry about getting enough protein on a vegetarian diet. There is a great deal of mythology surrounding protein. Many people assume that meat equals protein, which in turn equals health, and that we need a lot of protein and therefore need to eat meat. A lot of advertising for meat plays on this belief. Actually we can easily get the protein we need (45g a day for women, 55g for men,[53] although more is needed if pregnant or exercising heavily) from a vegetarian diet which includes nuts, seeds, pulses, and soya products – eaten daily. Dairy products and eggs are of course sources of protein for many vegetarians, although elsewhere in this book I have pointed out the ethical implications of eating these.

Although vegetarian diets may contain less protein, on average, than omnivorous diets, the British Nutrition Foundation's briefing paper on vegetarianism tells us 'there is *abundant* protein with a high overall amino acid score in most vegetarian diets' (my emphasis). Surveying a number of studies of protein intake in various groups, it concluded: 'In all cases, intakes of protein in vegetarians and in vegans appear fully sufficient in relation to estimated average requirements for protein.'[54] Just because there is less protein in a vegetarian diet does not mean there is not enough. Many top athletes, like tennis player Martina Navratilova, olympic gold hurdler Ed Moses, and cycling champion Sally Hibberd, are vegetarians. The list of famous vegetarian and vegan athletes includes bodybuilders, ice-skaters, basketball stars, runners, weight-lifters, and triathletes, showing that it is possible for the body to perform at peak effectiveness without meat.[55]

In fact, eating too much protein is bad for health. Diets very high in protein (in excess of 150g daily) cause calcium to be lost through the urine. This may explain why those who eat a lot of dairy products and meat are more likely to suffer osteoporosis than those who are vegetarian or vegan.[56] In addition, protein cannot be stored in the body in significant quantities. When we consume excess protein we convert it into carbohydrate, producing toxic nitrogenous waste products.

Having said that, those who are pregnant, or who participate in intensive physical activities, do need to eat more protein than the average person. But even the amounts of protein that bodybuilders require (and bodybuilders are fanatical about protein) are easily supplied by a vegetarian diet. The nutrition director of an internationally famous chain of body-building gyms said: 'I supervise 160 employees around the world who've probably worked with over 300 vegetarian bodybuilders. These employees report to me that the vegetarian bodybuilders are building muscle just as nicely as if they ate meat.'[57]

There is a persistent myth that meat proteins are 'first class' while proteins from vegetarian sources are 'second class'. This outdated view is based on the fact that meat and eggs contain all the amino acids (the building blocks of proteins) whereas no individual vegetable or pulse does, except soya. Twenty amino acids go to make up proteins. We can make many of these in the body by converting other amino acids, but there are eight that must be present in the diet. These are the 'essential amino acids'.

However, it turns out that when we eat rice or cereals in combination with pulses or nuts all the essential amino acids are present in the correct proportions. This means that many classic food combinations (rice and dhal, macaroni cheese, beans on toast, felafel with pitta bread, peanut butter sandwiches) give protein that is at least as high in quality as meat. However, it's not strictly necessary to combine proteins in every meal. We have a 'pool' of amino acids and if one amino acid is deficient we can make this up from our body's stores if we eat them all regularly.[58]

If you are unfortunate enough to suffer from serious health problems such as kidney or liver disease, it would be prudent to take medical advice before changing your diet. For healthy individuals, as long as you eat a vegetarian diet drawing on a variety of sources as indicated in the chart on page 56, you will be eating enough protein and giving your body all the amino acids it needs.

5

COMMONLY ASKED QUESTIONS

You may still have some questions – most people do
when they are considering changing their diet. This
section attempts to address some of the more common
questions.

How do I give up eating meat?

Nowadays it's remarkably easy to become vegetarian.
Indeed, it is easier now, in the West, than at any previous
time. Virtually every restaurant has a vegetarian selection on the menu. A few years ago, vegetarians had to
haunt health-food stores; now even the supermarkets
have latched on to the fact that the vegetarian population is substantial (7 per cent of young adults in the UK
in 1999) and enthusiastically market vegetarian products.

There has been an explosion in the number of cookery
books devoted exclusively to vegetarian food, and many
of these are remarkably inexpensive. Buy some. Look at
the pictures and try out some of the recipes. You may

realize that some of your favourite foods are vegetarian and you hadn't even thought about it! Many people imagine that a vegetarian meal is meat-and-two-veg with the meat missing, or replaced by some kind of soya substitute. Once you begin to explore vegetarian cookery you will begin to see that pattern as hopelessly limited and won't even try to imitate it most of the time. You can slowly build up a new repertoire of dishes, gradually phasing the meat out of your diet. Or you can just decide to stop eating meat right now.

Telling others what you are doing and why – kindly and clearly – can help you to reinforce it and clarify your thinking. Some will be supportive, others may be hostile (and may think they're being criticized even when they aren't). Those who might invite you to dinner need to know you're vegetarian or it might prove embarrassing for both of you. Let them know – it's really not a problem since most people by now must be used to catering for vegetarian friends. Anyone who wants to have guests round had better get used to catering for vegetarians, given that people are increasingly giving up meat.

If you're the only vegetarian in your family, that is more difficult, but not insurmountable. There are cookery books designed to help you and your family cope with this. In addition, supermarkets supply many vegetarian frozen and chilled foods (although it's a shame to eat mass-produced food when home-cooked is usually much better). You could try introducing the others in your family to the food you eat. They might be pleasantly surprised.

Surely it is impossible to live without causing harm?
It's true that it's impossible to live without causing any harm. Even the cultivation of vegetables and grains kills many small creatures living in the earth, and pesticides (whether organic or chemical) kill many insects. We should not dismiss this out of hand. If we wish to reduce the amount of suffering in the world, we should be aware of such issues.

However, some forms of agricultural practice cause less destruction than others. If we have a choice of foods grown in different ways, it would be sensible to choose those grown by the most ethically acceptable methods. At the very least, it would be good if we began to make more use of organically grown produce. The build-up of long-lasting toxic chemicals in the food chain undoubtedly leads to problems for birds and higher mammals (including ourselves), and we should discourage the use of such chemicals.

As an argument for meat-eating, though, the idea that we cannot avoid causing some harm simply does not hold water. There is *some* harm that we *can* avoid. The harm caused to farm animals is unnecessary, and we can, and indeed should, avoid it if we regard ourselves as compassionate. We may not be able to live without causing any harm at all but we can certainly live in such a way that we cause less harm.

Plants are living too. Aren't vegetarians inconsistent?
The notion that vegetarians are being inconsistent in eating plants because plants are living things is very

common: there can scarcely be a vegetarian who hasn't heard this argument several times. It is hard, however, to see how plants can suffer. They have nothing corresponding to a central nervous system or even to nerves. While it's of considerable evolutionary benefit for animals to have a sense of pain so that they can escape danger, why should plants, which are by nature static, have evolved such a sense? I believe that we instinctively recognize that plants are of a different order from animals. I doubt if many who employ the above argument would really feel the same seeing a carrot pulled out of the ground and eaten as they would seeing a lamb having its throat cut. The difference seems obvious.

A second count on which this argument falls is that it takes ten kilos of vegetable protein to produce one kilo of meat protein. Thus, by eating plants directly, rather than by converting them into animal protein first, we cause the deaths of far fewer of them. If you're concerned about causing less destruction to plants then become a vegetarian!

Why should I worry about animals when there is so much human suffering in the world?

For some, the issue of animal suffering is insignificant compared to the problems involved in human suffering. They would rather not, they say, divert their energies into preventing animals from suffering while there are so many humans in the world who lack food, medicine, and clean water.

If we had to make a choice between alleviating the sufferings of animals and that of humans, this argument would have a great deal of force. However, it is not necessary to do this. Becoming a vegetarian is not a difficult thing to do. It adds little or no extra demands to our lives. In choosing what to eat (something we have to do anyway) we simply choose to eat food that does not contain meat. In doing so we boycott a trade that leads to immeasurable suffering. The rest of our time is free to spend in whatever way we wish, including working for the welfare of other members of our species.

There is also a strong argument for becoming vegetarian to help other humans (apart from the many ecological arguments we've already looked at). The ten kilos of vegetable protein it takes to produce one of animal protein mean that raising animals is a vastly inefficient method of producing food. Animal farming has been correctly described as 'a protein factory in reverse'. As much as 40 per cent of the world's grain is used to feed cattle, pigs, and poultry.[59] In theory (for there are also problems of unequal distribution of wealth and food), we could feed many more people on a vegetarian diet. There would be far more food in the world to feed the hungry if we did not eat meat and potentially far less human suffering as a result.

How do I relate to meat-eaters?

Some meat-eaters seem to feel threatened when they are with a vegetarian. It is as if they sense an implied criticism in the simple action of someone asking if there is anything vegetarian on the menu. This may reveal an underlying sense of moral unease. We rarely acknowledge that meat is part of a dead animal, and nowadays meat is packaged to disguise the connection with the farm and slaughterhouse. Reminders of the connection are often unwelcome. It's therefore quite natural and to be expected that some meat-eaters will react in this way.

In return, some vegetarians can be self-righteous and harsh, but most are not. If a vegetarian is self-righteous, the problem is with their lack of metta, and not with their diet. They need to learn to have more respect and kindness towards others and not to judge harshly. If you are going to become a vegetarian it's good to be aware of any tendency you might have toward self-righteousness. You can then deal with it by reminding yourself that you once ate meat, and for the same reasons that others continue to eat meat. A little patience, kindness, and humility are called for.

What would happen to the animals if we all became vegetarian?

There is one other argument that comes up surprisingly often. Well, if the whole world decided simultaneously to stop eating meat, there would be an enormous crisis! However, common sense tells us that changes do not happen in such a way, except where there is a major panic over health, as with salmonella in eggs or the BSE scare. Vegetarianism has been growing in recent decades but in the way we would expect – in a relatively slow, steady, and progressive manner. When change happens in this way, farmers and the food industry adjust to suit the market. Fewer animals are bred, so the total number of farm animals declines. There is no question of us being lumbered with vast herds of animals roaming around the countryside.

Will I miss having meat in my diet?

To start with, the answer for many people is probably 'yes'. It would be normal for you to experience cravings for meat from time to time – but this will probably be just a passing phase and won't last very long. If you begin to have doubts about what you're doing then reflect on your reasons for becoming vegetarian in the first place. Think about what it is you're really giving up – your involvement in death and destruction. Think about the benefits of what you're doing, for yourself; the benefits for your health and for your conscience – and for others; the contribution you're making towards a better world.

We all hit times when our own actions seem insignificant in this very large and complex world of ours. In the chapter on 'Meat and Metta' (page 80) we'll see that the whole subcontinent of India became almost entirely vegetarian as a result of individuals giving up meat – and that was in a time and place where there were no mass media to spread ideas and information. At times when we feel discouraged, it's good to bear this in mind. Your actions are important. You are shaping the world whatever you do. Why not change it for the better?

Above all, enjoy the change in your diet. You'll be performing a highly positive action in giving up meat.

You'll probably get more pleasure from your food, you'll almost certainly be healthier, and you can be absolutely sure that there will be less suffering in the world as a result of your actions.

What about veganism?

A vegan diet is one that excludes all animal products, including dairy and eggs. In addition many vegans do not wear leather or wool, and avoid other products that contain ingredients derived from animals.

For some, becoming vegetarian is not enough. The sufferings of animals in the dairy and poultry industries are so great that many people feel they have to take a stand against it by abstaining from dairy products and eggs. Indeed, it's a perfectly logical step from vegetarianism to veganism. If we want to reduce the amount of harm that our needs and appetites cause, it is unhelpful to assume that because we've become vegetarian we've done all we can. Vegetarians need to avoid complacency, and the arguments in this book support the change from vegetarianism to veganism just as much as they do the change from meat-eating to vegetarianism.

As we have seen, the dairy and meat industries are, in reality, a single economic entity. Cows have to calve in order to lactate. Most of the calves (mainly the male ones) have no value except as meat. By supporting the dairy industry, we are also supporting the meat industry. It makes sense, considering what we have seen, to go the whole way and stop supporting both. This can involve a bit of scrutinizing of labels – eggs and milk are used in a large range of products, including biscuits, cakes, yoghurt, ice-cream, chocolate, etc., although there are vegan alternatives to all of these.

If you do decide to become vegan there is one nutrient that you do need to take special notice of – vitamin B_{12}. This is needed for the healthy production of blood and to maintain the nervous system. Meat and dairy products are rich sources, but vegetables have only traces of this vitamin. However, it is abundant in yeast extract and fermented foods like soy sauce and miso, and B_{12} is added as a supplement to other foods (some margarines, soya milk, breakfast cereals, etc.). We need only minute quantities every day, and even in pregnancy two-millionths of a gram daily should be sufficient for good health. If in doubt take a supplement.

If you eat meat, you might think it's too big a change to go straight to a vegan diet. In fact your digestive system might not take kindly to such a large change in your dietary habits in too short a time. It makes more sense to change your habits little by little – after all, any change you make in moving towards veganism is going to benefit the world. Even if you don't feel you can make the step from being a meat-eater to being a vegan all at once, it is still good to be aware that becoming vegetarian is an immensely positive action. It will lead, over the course of an average human life, to many scores of animals not having to experience the hells that we have been exploring in imagination. Once you feel comfortable about being a vegetarian you can begin to adopt a vegan diet more and more.

If you are a vegetarian who still eats dairy products and eggs, I hope this exploration of the principles of vegetarianism and the practices of modern farming will persuade you to take a further step in the direction of abstaining from harm and cultivating an all-embracing love for all that lives.

6

DID THE BUDDHA EAT MEAT?

I have suggested that the natural expression of a Buddhist ethical sensitivity is to become a vegetarian: that the natural outcome of a greater awareness of the reality of interconnectedness is that we will experience more compassion. With a deeper experience of compassion, we will want to avoid unnecessary suffering and will stop eating meat. However, I've also pointed out that not all Buddhists are vegetarian and that many claim that the Buddha himself ate meat. So what is the truth? Does Buddhism really support the practice of vegetarianism?

There are a number of passages in the early Buddhist scriptures suggesting that the Buddha and his monastic followers were meat-eaters. One of the most often quoted is from a teaching called the *Jivaka Sutta*:

> I say that in three situations flesh can be partaken of –
> when it is not seen, heard, or suspected (that an animal
> has been killed for a monk).[60]

Although some have argued that this might be a later interpolation by meat-eating monks, there are many passing references to meat-eating amongst monks and nuns, carried out with the Buddha's knowledge and without his condemnation.[61] I would argue that the Buddha certainly did eat meat.

What are we to make of this? Doesn't it go against the whole case we have built for vegetarianism based on the first precept? Was the Buddha ignoring his own ethical teachings? If the Buddha ate meat is it permissible for us to follow suit? These are all bracing questions but it's impossible to begin exploring them without first looking at the social context in which the Buddha and his monks and nuns were practising. It is only by looking at the nature of early Buddhist monasticism and the prevailing dietary habits of the population at large that we can understand why the Buddha allowed meat-eating.

Firstly, Buddhist monks and nuns were mendicants; that is, they begged for their food from householders. The word *bhikkhu*, or monk (the feminine is *bhikkhuni*), comes from a root that means 'to beg'. The monastic code did not allow them to grow their own food but to accept only food that someone else gave them. There were important reasons for monks and nuns to follow these rules. They could not grow their own food because that would inevitably result in them causing harm to the small creatures that live in the ground.[62] For a monk to consciously kill any living creature was a grave breach of the principle of metta, or non-harm.[63] The monastic code prevented monks and nuns from even using water containing microscopic creatures[64] and from making bricks from mud lest they kill any of the creatures living in it.[65] The monastic rules demanded the thorough practice of non-harm and metta – as we would expect, given how fundamental these ideas are in Buddhist ethics. Monks and nuns were even allowed from compassion to free animals from hunters' traps – even though that would normally be viewed as theft.[66] How then could these practitioners of non-harm eat meat?

In the early years of the Buddhist monastic tradition many – probably nearly all – of the householders from whom the monks and nuns begged would eat meat. Few of those householders – and none in the earliest days – would have been Buddhist. Much of the food offered would not have been vegetarian. In those days the custom of the monks was not to remain settled but to travel widely to spread the Dharma. Only during the rainy months would they live in shelters and remain in one place. During the remainder of the year the monks and nuns would often have entered villages new to them and would not know the people who gave them food, or whether they were vegetarian.

Householders believed they could gain merit by offering food to religious mendicants, and through this have a better rebirth. An important role of the monk was to allow householders (of whatever religious persuasion) to gain merit in this way. It was the duty of monks and nuns to be the recipient of alms and to give householders the opportunity to gain merit. A monk was 'morally bound to accept any alms offered in good faith by a pious donor and that if he failed to do so he was interfering with the karmic fruit and just reward that the donor was entitled to expect'.[67] Therefore, even if a gift was not vegetarian, it was a monk's duty to accept the donation. It would have been considered very bad manners to refuse unless there was a very good reason to do so. In fact, refusing an offering of food was used to punish a householder who had falsely accused a monk or nun of wrongdoing.[68]

Monks and nuns were simply not able to be vegetarian without great difficulty. This is why the Buddha ate meat, and allowed his monastic followers to eat meat as well. Other mendicant religious practitioners appear to have been in the same position. Nowadays followers of the Jain religion[69] in India are strictly vegetarian, yet the Jaina scriptures – which describe the same period in Indian history as the early Buddhist scriptures – reveal that their mendicants too ate meat.[70] This reinforces the suggestion that it was very difficult, in the early days of Buddhism, to obtain vegetarian food.

The Buddha also *allowed* monks and nuns, of course, to be vegetarian, although he specifically refused to make the practice compulsory. Significantly, being vegetarian was seen as an ascetic practice along with other austerities such as sleeping only beneath trees or wearing only cast-off rags. The fact that living on a vegetarian diet was considered an ascetic practice of this sort suggests that it might have been a very difficult thing to do at that time and in that social context. There was one occasion when monks or nuns could specifically request meat, and this was when they were ill. One wonders if this was a recognition that trying to live on scraps might result in malnutrition. Presumably trying to assemble a healthy vegetarian meal out of the same leftovers would be even harder.

Bhikkhus and bhikkhunis, of course, were not the only Buddhists. There were also lay followers of the Buddha. The householders were, as we would expect, in a different position from the monks and nuns. They worked for a living rather than begged, and had a choice in what they ate. Just as the laity supported the monks and nuns materially, the monks and nuns supported the laity spiritually, through teaching them. Teachings given by monks and nuns to laypeople, particularly the ethical teachings that encouraged non-harm and the practice of metta, would have encouraged them to give up meat-eating, along with livelihoods that caused harm. Once, when a gathering of lay disciples came to visit the Buddha, he told them:

> Now I will tell you of the rules of conduct for a householder, according to which, he becomes a good disciple.... Let him not destroy life nor cause others to destroy life and, also, not approve of others' killing. Let him refrain from oppressing all living beings in the world, whether strong or weak.[71]

This teaching clearly encouraged the laity to give up meat. Following this teaching a lay follower could not be a 'good disciple' of the Buddha and kill animals for food, nor could he buy meat. For how could one buy meat from a butcher without approving of his killing? In buying meat from a butcher, we are financially rewarding him for his unethical activity. If we were to look for vegetarianism among the early Buddhists, it seems clear that we would most likely find it among householders.

Buddhism presents us then with an apparently paradoxical situation where the early monks and nuns, who were not vegetarian, would have been encouraging householders to give up eating meat. Those vegetarian Buddhist householders would have been offering food that did not contain meat to the monastics. At first, of course, the proportion of the population that was vegetarian would have been too small to have had much impact on a monk's consumption of meat. Nevertheless, over time it would have had an enormous impact, since Buddhism became widespread in the centuries after the Buddha's death. We do have evidence that a few hundred years after the death of the Buddha vegetarianism had increasingly become the norm.

So why did the Buddha tell monks and nuns they could eat meat if they did not see, hear, or suspect that a householder had killed an animal especially for their benefit? It seems quite likely that householders living in a largely non-vegetarian country would have seen meat as a special food. If meat was special it would make a special offering for a religious beggar. Giving a special offering might confer special merit, leading to a better rebirth. So it is quite possible that there would be a minor outbreak of slaughtering accompanying the arrival of religious mendicants in a village. We know from later

Buddhist sources that this did happen.[72] It would be akin to the practice – still common in India to this day – of making an animal sacrifice.[73] This would be something that the Buddha – interested in advocating the principle of metta – would not want to encourage. It was important that monastics too did not encourage others to kill, or approve of their killing. If a monastic knowingly accepted such meat he or she would be condoning the slaughter of animals as offerings. Hence the injunction that monks and nuns had to be alert to any signs that an animal had been specially killed for them.

7

MEAT AND METTA

How does all this affect us in the modern West? Many
lay Buddhists eat meat. They say that since the meat they
buy in the supermarket, restaurant, or butcher's shop
was not killed specially for them they are merely following the Buddha's teaching. If we are living a mendicant
lifestyle – begging as the Buddha and his bhikkhus did
– then we can indeed justify eating meat. We would still,
however, have to make sure that we were not encouraging anyone to cause harm. We would be duty-bound to
ensure that no one was killing animals for our benefit,
and should be encouraging the development of metta
and the practice of vegetarianism. However, few of us
are in that position, except for the minority who live a
mendicant lifestyle.

Most of us are in the position of the early Buddhist
householders. Therefore, our guidelines regarding meat-
eating should not be a teaching implemented for the
benefit of monks and nuns who lived by begging. If we

are not begging in this way then we can't apply the notion of it being ethically acceptable to eat meat if the animal hasn't been killed specifically for us. This practice only makes sense within a context of the practice of mendicancy. Instead, as householders, we should follow the teachings that exhort us 'not to kill, or cause to kill, or approve of others killing'. By giving up eating meat we stop 'causing to kill' since we are taking away the demand to satisfy our old appetite. We are also not 'approving of others killing' by stopping giving financial rewards to the seller of meat and the people who kill the animals. We are practising, in effect, a form of economic boycott of an unethical industry.

Our actions have consequences. Where we have a choice we should choose the option with the most positive outcome. If we are aware that our actions are resulting in harm, we should change the way we act wherever it is feasible. Not to do so is unethical.

A few Buddhists do beg for their food in the West today. One monk I talked to has begged many times in this way, although he modifies traditional practice somewhat. He stands in the street near some shops holding his covered bowl. People come up and ask what he is doing, often assuming that he is begging for money. He explains that he is begging for food and that he can only accept food that is readily edible, as he cannot store it or cook it. If they ask what sort of food he prefers he will suggest something vegetarian. However, unsolicited food may contain meat. Interestingly, many people assume that since he is a Buddhist monk he must be vegetarian!

That particular bhikkhu actively encourages vegetarianism on the grounds of the first precept, but does on occasion receive donations of meat. The monastic rules allow him to leave aside anything he does not wish to eat. Sometimes, though, it is impossible to avoid meat, either because it is mixed in, or the meal offered is mostly meat. He follows a middle way – eating meat when it is unavoidable, and encouraging donors and lay Buddhists in particular to practise vegetarianism.[74]

Eating meat as an unavoidable consequence of a mendicant lifestyle is, I believe, an authentic way of practising the Dharma while not being a strict vegetarian. It is also in accord with the practice of the Buddha. The important point is that monks and nuns are, where at all possible, teaching their donors the principle of metta and its application of non-harm, and are encouraging them to be vegetarian, or at least to offer vegetarian food.

Unfortunately, for many monks and nuns in the east, and for some in the West, meat-eating is simply an unquestioned habit. Because they themselves eat meat it does not occur to them to encourage their donors to be vegetarian. They have forgotten, in this respect, to apply the principle of non-harm. Some monastics, like anyone else who eats meat, develop a sort of addiction to it. Apparently, some of the monks attending the 2,500th anniversary celebrations of the Buddha's birth protested about being given only vegetarian food by the Indian government.[75]

Closer to home, I have visited a Tibetan temple in Europe where meat is on sale in a shop in the temple grounds. Tibet is, to some extent, a special case, since it is very hard to be vegetarian there due to the poor climatic and agricultural conditions. Although vegetarianism is not very practical in Tibet it is still highly regarded and many Tibetans will take up vows of abstinence from meat for specific periods. However, when Tibetans come to the West and continue to eat meat, and do not encourage others to give it up, it appears that they are sadly neglecting the practice of the first precept. One lama living in the West declared, 'We Tibetans like to eat meat!'[76] as if the strength of his desire for meat precluded argument.

We have no way of knowing for sure whether the dynamic I've suggested – of vegetarianism growing in Buddhist culture as meat-eating monks and nuns encouraged householders to stop eating meat – is definitely what happened; the historical sources are simply too patchy. However, the hypothesis does fit the known facts.

The earliest record of an association between Buddhism and vegetarianism comes from King Ashoka, who lived about 250 years after the Buddha. After his conversion to Buddhism he tried to influence Indian society to be more compassionate, often leading by example. He proclaimed his exhortations on a series of messages carved into rocks and pillars throughout his kingdom. In one of those messages he reveals that his palace is becoming vegetarian:

> Hundreds of thousands of living creatures were
> formerly slaughtered every day for curries in the

> kitchens of his Majesty, Beloved of the Gods, of Sweet
> Countenance. As this edict is being inscribed, only three
> living beings are killed daily: two peacocks and one
> deer. And the deer is not slaughtered regularly. In the
> future, not even these three animals will be
> slaughtered.[77]

As well as being a fascinating snapshot of a monarch's attempt to introduce vegetarianism to his palace, this is the first evidence we have of Buddhists becoming vegetarian after the time of the Buddha. This also confirms that vegetarianism was associated with early Buddhist practice. And interestingly it is a layman (a monarch is still a layman) who is practising and propagating it. This fits with the hypothesis that it was the householders who were free to stop eating meat, and that they did so with the encouragement of their religious teachers.

I've already suggested that although monks and nuns ate meat they would at the same time advocate vegetarianism. Evidently, householders could also take on this role (in early Buddhism laypeople could also be teachers and sometimes had large numbers of followers). We can only assume that this promotion of vegetarianism was very successful, since several centuries later we learn from the records of Chinese monks visiting India that virtually the whole of India was now vegetarian. One of those monks wrote:

> The people of this country kill no living creatures.... The
> single exception to this is the Chandalas, who are
> known as 'evil men'.... Neither pigs nor fowl are kept in

this country and no living creatures are sold. There are no butchers or wine-sellers in the markets.... Only the Chandala fishermen and hunters sell flesh.[78]

Some of this may be an exaggeration, but if it is, presumably the exaggeration contains a truth – that vegetarianism was common, if not universal, in India at that time.

There is of course a certain tension involved in having meat-eating monks and nuns encouraging householders to be vegetarian. Monastics were supposed not to become attached to food, but (as we all know) it is very easy to become habitually used to eating certain foods. If vegetarianism began to spread in the wider population, monks and nuns who had something of an addiction to the meat in their begging-bowls would find themselves in conflict. They would be cutting off the source of their meat supply! We might also expect to find other monastics feeling that if they encouraged householders to be vegetarian they ought to follow the same practice themselves. Some polarization is to be expected. In fact, there seems to be evidence for this very thing.

The Mahayana – literally the 'greater way to Enlightenment' – saw itself as a reform movement. It emerged as a challenge to some rigid and literalistic tendencies that had emerged in early Buddhism. It emphasized the spirit of Buddhism – the spirit of compassion – over the following of rules in a literal manner (including rules that allowed you to eat meat!). Vegetarianism, as we might expect, is more widely practised in the Mahayana Buddhist traditions. The *Lankavatara Sutra*[79] is a relatively late Buddhist text from the Mahayana scriptures.

An entire chapter of this sutra is dedicated to advocating vegetarianism,[80] and shows the existence of a tension between those monks who adopted a vegetarian diet and those who continued to eat meat.

In the *Lankavatara Sutra* the link between the first precept and vegetarianism is clear:

> The Bodhisattva, whose nature is compassion, is not to eat any meat.… For fear of causing terror to living beings … let the Bodhisattva who is disciplining himself to attain compassion, refrain from eating flesh.[81]

There are also arguments explicitly against the *Jivaka Sutta*. The *Lankavatara* argues:

> It is not true … that meat is proper food and permissible … when (the victim) was not killed by himself, when he did not order others to kill it, when it was not specially meant for him.[82]

It seems then that a polarization of Buddhists into those who give the first precept priority over the *Jivaka Sutta* and those who give the *Jivaka Sutta* priority over the first precept was established by perhaps a thousand years after the Buddha. This polarization, as we have seen, still exists today. As the benefit of a historical perspective was lacking to those earlier Buddhists we can see how it can be true both that the Buddha ate meat and that the first precept implies vegetarianism.

CONCLUSION

The Buddha's teaching of the principle of metta, in the midst of a culture where the population commonly sacrificed animals and ate meat, caused a radical change that has survived in India to this day. The practice of the monks and nuns eating whatever was offered, while encouraging householders to give up eating meat, bore fruit. The historical record, as shown in the edicts of Ashoka, the writings of Chinese visitors to India, and in later Mahayana sutras, shows a progressive spread of vegetarianism alongside the growth of Buddhism.

Those who argue that Buddhists – following the *Jivaka Sutta* – should eat meat cannot explain the rapid growth of vegetarianism that paralleled the expansion of Buddhism from the earliest days. Vegetarianism is honoured, if not always practised, in virtually every Buddhist country. In fact over time China and Japan became almost entirely vegetarian because of Buddhist practice.[83] The movement started by the Buddha had a profound effect on the habits of almost a third of the world's population. Many millions of animals' lives must have been saved and untold suffering prevented by the radical application of Buddhist ethics. How inspiring it is that the cumulative ethical actions of individuals can shape entire cultures!

This process of sensitization to suffering can, with encouragement, be repeated. We can change the world. It is my aspiration that the practice of the first precept will become thorough and widespread in the West, and that the principle of metta will spread through the world in an ever-widening circle. May we all strive to cultivate a boundless heart and learn to live in love and compassion toward all that lives.

NOTES AND REFERENCES

1 Peter Singer, *Animal Liberation*, Random House, London 1995, p.108.

2 *Animal Liberation*, op. cit., p.105.

3 *Veterinary Record* vol.iii no.2, 1982. Quoted in Kath Clements, *Why Vegan*, Heretic, London 1995, p.56.

4 'Piggy in the middle', *New Scientist*, 23 January 1999, accessed 1 April 1999; available on-line at: http://www.newscientist.com/ns/19990123/newsstory10.html.

5 *Animal Liberation*, op. cit., p.173.

6 John Bennett, *The Hunger Machine*, Polity, Cambridge 1987, p.37.

7 H. Saddhatissa (trans.), *Sutta Nipata*, Curzon, London 1985, p.34.

8 Farm Animal Welfare Council, *Report on the Welfare of Livestock (Red Meat Animals) at the Time of Slaughter*, HMSO, London 1984, paragraphs 88 and 124.

9 *Agscene*, no.128, Winter 1997, p.13.

10 *Animal Liberation*, op. cit., p.152.

11 See, for example, the Ministry of Agriculture, Fisheries

and Food's *Response* to the *Report on the Welfare of Livestock (Red Meat Animals) at the Time of Slaughter*, MAFF, Surbiton 1985, pp.7–8, where the pros and cons are discussed.

12 *Genesis* 1:26.

13 *Genesis* 9:2–3.

14 Thomas Aquinas, *Summa Theologica*. Christian Classics, Westminster 1981, p.1282.

15 J.P. Mahaffy, *Descartes*, Blackwood, Edinburgh 1880, p.181.

16 Fernand van Steenberghen, *Hidden God*, Publications Universitaires de Louvain, Belgium 1966, p.252.

17 *New Scientist*, 25 April 1992, accessed 1 April 1999, available on-line at: http://www.newscientist.com/nsplus/insight/animal/pain.html.

18 Kate Crosby and Andrew Skilton, *The Bodhicaryavatara*, Oxford University Press, Oxford 1995, p.96.

19 See Alex Kennedy, *The Buddhist Vision*, Rider, London 1985, for a detailed account of this symbol.

20 A particularly good example is the children's book, *The Monkey King*, written and illustrated by Adiccabandhu and Padmasri, Windhorse, Birmingham 1998.

21 *See* P.D. Ryan, *Buddhism and the Natural World*, Windhorse, Birmingham 1998, for further explorations of the relationship between Buddhism and animals.

22 Sohaku Ogata (trans.) *The Transmission of the Lamp: Early Masters*, Longwood Academic, Durango, Colorado 1991.

23 Juan Mascaro, *Dhammapada*, Penguin, London 1973, p.54.

24 Many farmers are very unhappy about the way modern farming has developed. Unfortunately, the realities of the market place mean that people want cheap meat. And since intensive farming is the most economic way of

achieving this, if farmers wish to remain in business they have to mistreat their animals.

25 Sangharakshita, *A Guide to the Buddhist Path*, Windhorse, Birmingham 1996, p.179.

26 John D. Ireland, *The Udana: Inspired Utterances of the Buddha*, Buddhist Publication Society, Kandy 1990, p.73.

27 Although this formulation is often called the 'threefold way', the term *trishiksha* literally means 'threefold training'.

28 Every Buddhist precept can be said to have two aspects – what we abstain from (expressed, for example, in the list of five or ten precepts) and what we attempt to practise (expressed in the lists of *dharmas*, or positive ethical actions). Traditionally more attention is given to reminding ourselves of abstention, but I have given both formulations here. In the 112th sutta of the 'Middle Length Sayings' the relationship between abstention and action is clear. 'I lived having renounced the destruction of life, and with the stick thrown aside, weapon-free, scrupulous, compassionate, friendly and kind of heart towards all living things.' (David W. Evans (trans.), *The Discourses of Gautama Buddha: Middle Collection*, Janus, London 1991, p.348). For more on the five precepts and corresponding *dharmas*, see Abhaya, *Living the Skilful Life*, Windhorse, Birmingham 1996.

29 *Dhammapada*, op. cit., p.54.

30 Kamalashila, *Meditation: the Buddhist Way of Tranquillity and Insight*, Windhorse, Birmingham 1996, and Paramananda, *Change Your Mind*, Windhorse, Birmingham 1996, are full and practical guides to the practices mentioned here.

31 P.B. Shelley, *In Defence of Poetry*.

32 *Animal Liberation*, op. cit., p.166.

33 Peter Singer, *How Are We to Live?*, Prometheus, Amherst NY 1995, p.44.

34 ibid., p.45.

35 S. Tamminga, 'Gaseous Pollutants Produced by Farm Animal Enterprises', in Clive Phillips and David Piggins (eds.), *Farm Animals and the Environment*, CAB International, Wallingford 1992, p.347.

36 *Farm Animals and the Environment*, op. cit., p.325, quotes statistics from the National Rivers Authority showing an average 3–4,000 incidents of water pollution from farms annually.

37 *Animal Liberation*, op. cit., p.168, reports 3,500 incidents of water pollution in 1985, just one of which – involving one farm – caused the deaths of 110,000 fish.

38 Clive Phillips and David Piggins, 'Effects of Farm Animals on the Environment', in *Farm Animals and the Environment*, op. cit., p.326.

39 Peter Cox, *Why You Don't Need Meat*, Bloomsbury, London 1992, p.45.

40 Frank P. Mathews and Robert J. Rubin, 'Influenza', *Colliers Encyclopedia*, Colliers, New York 1996, vol.13, p.16.

41 'The pigs must die', *New Scientist*, 3 April 1999, accessed 3 April 1999. Available on-line at: http://www.newscientist.com/ns/19990403/newsstory1.html

42 In 1997, six million pigs had to be slaughtered in the Netherlands to control a major epidemic of Classical Swine Fever which, fortunately for us, is not transmissible to humans. 'This little piggy fell ill', *New Scientist*, 12 September 1998. Accessed 1 April 1999.

Available on-line at: http://www.newscientist.com/ns/980912/nfocus.html

43 'Intensive farming methods "risk to health"', *Guardian*, 12 March 1998, p.6.

44 *Vegetarianism*, British Nutrition Foundation, London 1995, p.4.

45 *Why You Don't Need Meat*, op. cit., p.7.

46 'Eat less red meat to cut cancer risk, urges report,' *Guardian*, 26 September 1997.

47 Atherosclerosis: Hardening and thickening of the arteries accompanied by fatty degeneration – a common sign of heart disease associated in humans with over-consumption of saturated fats.

48 *Why You Don't Need Meat*, op. cit., p.148.

49 American Dietetic Association, *Vegetarian Diets* (accessed 6 April 1999). Available on-line at http://www.eatright. org/adap1197.html.

50 *Vegetarianism*, op. cit., p.15.

51 ibid., p.22.

52 *Why You Don't Need Meat*, op. cit., p.153.

53 Vegetarian Society information sheet, *Basic Nutrition*, (no date) accessed 1 April 1999. Available on-line at: http://www.vegsoc.org/Info/basnutr.html.

54 *Vegetarianism*, op. cit., p.10.

55 An extensive list of vegan and vegetarian athletes of national and international stature is available on-line at: http://veggie.org/veggie/famous.veg.athletes.html

56 Vegetarian Society information sheet, *Calcium*, accessed 1 April 1999. Available on-line at: http://www.vegsoc. org/info/calcium.html.

57 'Where's the Beef? Vegetarian bodybuilders show there's

more than one way to feed growing muscle', *Muscle and Fitness*, October 1992, p.130.

58 Vegetarian Society information sheet, *Basic Nutrition*, (no date) accessed 1 April 1999. Available on-line at: http://www.vegsoc.org/info/basnutr.html.

59 John Bennett, *The Hunger Machine*, Polity Press, Cambridge 1987, p.37.

60 *The Discourses of Gautama Buddha: Middle Collection*, op.cit., p.162.

61 In many cases, the meat-eating is simply part of the background in a tale that has no bearing on diet at all. There is a story where the enlightened nun Uppalavanna offers meat to the Buddha (I.B. Horner (trans.), *Book of the Discipline*, Part 2, Pali Text Society, London 1982, pp.36–8). There is another where the monk Upananda is rebuked for accepting money instead of meat (ibid., p.99), and an incident where the Buddha allows monks and nuns to ask specifically for meat when they are ill (ibid., p.342). There are many other examples.

62 I.B. Horner (trans.) *Book of the Discipline*, Part 2, Pali Text Society, London 1982, p.223.

63 *Book of the Discipline*, Part 3, 1983, p.1: 'Whatever monk should intentionally deprive a living thing of life, there is an offence.'

64 Mohan Wijayaratna, *Buddhist Monastic Life*, Cambridge University Press, Cambridge 1990, p.70.

65 *Book of the Discipline*, Part 1, 1992, p.65.

66 *Book of the Discipline*, Part 1, op. cit., p.105.

67 D. Seyfort Ruegg, 'Ahimsa and Vegetarianism in the History of Buddhism', in Balasooriya (ed.), *Buddhist Studies in Honour of Walpola Rahula*, Gordon Fraser,

London 1980, p.239.

68 *Buddhist Monastic Life*, op. cit., p.128.

69 Jains belong to a religious tradition founded by
Mahavira, who was an elder contemporary of the
Buddha. Jain monastics took non-harm to greater lengths
than the Buddhists, even to the point of starving
themselves to death in order to avoid causing harm.

70 Max Müller (ed.), *Sacred Books of the East vol.xxii, Gaina
Suttas*, trans. Hermann Jacobi, Oxford University Press,
Oxford 1895, pp.114–5: 'A monk or nun on a begging tour
may be invited to meat or fish containing many bones …
he should say, after consideration "…if you want to give
me a portion of whatever size, give it me; but not the
bones!"' and p.300: 'He may accept one donation of salt
for seasoning his meat.'

71 H. Saddhatissa (trans.) *Sutta Nipata*, Curzon, London
1985, p.44.

72 Lama Shabkar wrote a poem where goats and sheep
complain about this practice:
   *When some lamas enter someone's house
   And seat themselves comfortably upon the throne,
   We are being slaughtered right outside the door –
   Don't pretend you don't know what's going on!*
Excerpted from *The Life of Shabkar: The Autobiography of a
Tibetan Yogin*, quoted in *Tricycle*, Winter 1994, p.62.

73 Animal sacrifice was another common practice against
which the Buddha campaigned.

74 This particular monk was a vegetarian until taking
ordination. He started eating meat once he became a
monk, and did not enjoy the experience!

75 Sangharakshita, unpublished seminar transcript.

76 *Tricycle*, Winter 1994, p.56.

77 Christopher Chapple, 'Nonviolence to Animals in Buddhism and Jainism', in Kenneth Kraft (ed.), *Inner Peace, World Peace*, SUNY, New York 1992, p.55.

78 Fa-hsien (trans. Li Yung-hsi), *A Record of the Buddhist Countries*, Chinese Buddhist Association, Peking 1957, p.35. (The Chandalas were, and still are, regarded as being the most 'impure' of the untouchable groups in the Hindu social system.)

79 Mahayana scriptures are known as 'sutras', which is Sanskrit, rather than 'suttas', which is the equivalent Pali word.

80 Some commentators believe this chapter to be a later addition, but this does not affect our argument.

81 D.T. Suzuki (trans.), *Lankavatara Sutra*, SMC, Taipei 1991, pp.212–3.

82 ibid., p.217.

83 G.P. Malalasekara (ed.), *Encyclopaedia of Buddhism*, Government of Ceylon, Colombo 1961, p.291, writing about vegetarianism in China, says: 'From this time onwards [early sixth century] the eating of meat gradually ceased, and this tended to become general.'

FURTHER READING

BUDDHIST ETHICS

Abhaya, *Living the Skilful Life*, Windhorse, Birmingham 1996

Philip Kapleau, *To Cherish All Life*, Zen Center,
    Rochester NY 1986

Sangharakshita, *The Ten Pillars of Buddhism*, Windhorse,
    Birmingham 1996

VEGETARIANISM

Kath Clements, *Why Vegan*, Heretic, London 1995

Peter Cox, *Why You Don't Need Meat*, Bloomsbury,
    London 1992

Victoria Moran, *Compassion, The Ultimate Ethic:
    An Exploration of Veganism*, Thorsons, 1985

Peter Singer, *Animal Liberation*, Random House, London 1995

INDEX

A

abattoir 22ff
alms 75, 78, 81
anaemia 58
animals
　Buddhist view 30
　consciousness 28
　sacrifice 79
antibiotics 54
Aquinas, Thomas 27
Ashoka 83, 87
athletes 60
awareness 41, 46

B

bacteria 53
begging 75, 81
behaviourism 29
bhikkhu(ni) 74ff
broilers 17
BSE 53

Buddha 42
　eating meat 73ff
Buddhist views 25
Buddhist scriptures 73ff

C

calcium 59
calves 12ff
cattle 11ff
chickens 15ff
　free-range 16
cholera 53
Christianity 26ff
compassion 41, 86
conditioned co-production 38
conscience 36, 46
Creutzfeldt-Jakob disease 53

D

dairy farming 11ff
dairy industry 70

Dalai Lama 7
dehorning 13
Descartes 28
Dhammapada 33, 36, 43, 45
diet 55ff

E
empathy 39, 42, 44, 48
environmental issues 50ff
epidemics 53
ethics 8, 42ff, 81

F
farming 11ff
fish 21

G
Genesis 27
global warming 51
guilt 39

H
happiness 40
harm 45, 65
health 54ff
heart disease 58, 93

I
imagination 47
immeasurables 46
India 69, 84
Indra 22
influenza 53
insight 43, 47
interconnectedness 36ff, 46
iron 56, 58

J
Jains 76, 95
Jatakas 31
Jivaka Sutta 73, 86

K
karuna 41
killing 22ff, 34, 80

L
laity 77
Lankavatara Sutra 85
love 40, 44, 46

M
Mahavira 95
meat-eating 25ff, 34, 57
meditation 43, 46
merit 78
metta 40ff, 45, 87
metta bhavana 46
mindfulness of breathing 46
monastic code 74, *see also*
  precepts
mudita 41

N
Noah 27

O
offerings *see* alms
osteoporosis 59, 61

P
pathogens 52
pigs 17ff, 53

plague 53
poultry industry 70 *see also*
    chickens
pratitya-samutpada 38
precepts 43, *see also*
    monastic code
protein 56, 59ff

R
rebirth 31

S
Sangharakshita 39
scriptures, Jaina 76
self-righteousness 68
sheep 20f
Shelley, P.B. 47, 48
Skinner, B.F. 29
stunning 22
suffering 30
sympathetic joy 41

T
Tao-lin 33
threefold way 91
Tibet 83
trishiksha 91

U
Upananda 94
Uppalavanna 94

V
veal 14
veganism 70
views 25
    Buddhist 30
    Christian 26
viruses 53
vitamin B_{12} 56, 71

W
Wheel of Life 30

The Windhorse symbolizes the energy of the enlightened mind carrying the Three Jewels – the Buddha, the Dharma, and the Sangha – to all sentient beings.

Buddhism is one of the fastest-growing spiritual traditions in the Western world. Throughout its 2,500-year history, it has always succeeded in adapting its mode of expression to suit whatever culture it has encountered.

Windhorse Publications aims to continue this tradition as Buddhism comes to the West. Today's Westerners are heirs to the entire Buddhist tradition, free to draw instruction and inspiration from all the many schools and branches. Windhorse publishes works by authors who not only understand the Buddhist tradition but are also familiar with Western culture and the Western mind.

For orders and catalogues contact

WINDHORSE PUBLICATIONS	WINDHORSE BOOKS	WEATHERHILL INC
11 PARK ROAD	P O BOX 574	41 MONROE TURNPIKE
BIRMINGHAM	NEWTON	TRUMBULL
B13 8AB	NSW 2042	CT 06611
UK	AUSTRALIA	USA

Windhorse Publications is an arm of the Friends of the Western Buddhist Order, which has more than sixty centres on five continents. Through these centres, members of the Western Buddhist Order offer regular programmes of events for the general public and for more experienced students. These include meditation classes, public talks, study on Buddhist themes and texts, and 'bodywork' classes such as t'ai chi, yoga, and massage. The FWBO also runs several retreat centres and the Karuna Trust, a fund-raising charity that supports social welfare projects in the slums and villages of India.

Many FWBO centres have residential spiritual communities and ethical businesses associated with them. Arts activities are encouraged too, as is the development of strong bonds of friendship between people who share the same ideals. In this way the FWBO is developing a unique approach to Buddhism, not simply as a set of techniques, less still as an exotic cultural interest, but as a creatively directed way of life for people living in the modern world.

If you would like more information about the FWBO please write to

LONDON BUDDHIST CENTRE	ARYALOKA
51 ROMAN ROAD	HEARTWOOD CIRCLE
LONDON	NEWMARKET
E2 0HU	NH 03857
UK	USA

ALSO FROM WINDHORSE

PARAMANANDA

CHANGE YOUR MIND:
A PRACTICAL GUIDE TO BUDDHIST MEDITATION

Buddhism is based on the truth that, with effort, we can change the way we are. But how? Among the many methods Buddhism has to offer, meditation is the most direct. It is the art of getting to know one's own mind and learning to encourage what is best in us.

This is an accessible and thorough guide to meditation, based on traditional material but written in a light and modern style. Colourfully illustrated with anecdotes and tips from the author's experience as a meditator and teacher, it also offers refreshing inspiration to seasoned meditators.

208 pages, with photographs
ISBN 0 904766 81 0
£8.99/$17.95

SANGHARAKSHITA

THE TEN PILLARS OF BUDDHISM

The Ten Pillars of Buddhism are ten ethical principles which together provide a comprehensive guide to the moral dimension of human life.

To explore them is to turn the lens of moral vision on to one aspect of life after another. To apply them is to accept the challenge of human potential for higher development – and to work with that challenge in the arena of everyday life.

Readers from the Buddhist world will find some of Sangharakshita's ideas especially thought-provoking – and even controversial. But all readers, whether Buddhists or not, will find this essay an invaluable source of stimulation and insight in their quest for ethical standards by which to live.

112 pages
ISBN 1 899579 21 4
£5.99/$11.95

SANGHARAKSHITA

A GUIDE TO THE BUDDHIST PATH

Which Buddhist teachings really matter? How does one begin to practise them in a systematic way? Without a guide one can easily get dispirited or lost.

In this highly readable anthology a leading Western Buddhist sorts out fact from myth, essence from cultural accident, to reveal the fundamental ideals and teachings of Buddhism. The result is a reliable map of the Buddhist path that anyone can follow.

Sangharakshita is an ideal companion on the path. As founder of a major Western Buddhist movement he has helped thousands of people to make an effective contact with the richness and beauty of the Buddha's teachings.

256 pages, with illustrations
ISBN 1 899579 04 4
£12.50/$24.95

P.D. RYAN

BUDDHISM AND THE NATURAL WORLD:
TOWARDS A MEANINGFUL MYTH

P.D. Ryan takes a fresh look at our relationship with the living world and offers a radical analysis of our consumerist attitudes. Applying the Buddha's fundamental message of non-violence to these crucial issues, he draws out a middle way between destructiveness and sentimentality: a way which recognizes the truth of the interdependence of all life and places universal compassion at the very centre of our relationship with the world.

In *Buddhism and the Natural World* Ryan emphasizes the importance of living in accord with this truth – and reminds us of the Buddha's insistence that to do so calls for nothing less than a revolution in consciousness.

144 pages
ISBN 1 899579 00 1
£6.99/$13.95